THE GARDEN OF THE PLYNCK

Karle Wilson Baker

1st WORLD
LIBRARY
Literary Society

The Garden of the Plynck

Karle Wilson Baker

© 1st World Library, 2006
PO Box 2211
Fairfield, IA 52556
www.1stworldlibrary.com
First Edition

LCCN: 2006907715

Softcover ISBN: 1-4218-2441-8
Hardcover ISBN: 1-4218-2341-1
eBook ISBN: 1-4218-2541-4

Purchase *"The Garden of the Plynck"*
as a traditional bound book at:
www.1stWorldLibrary.com/purchase.asp?ISBN=1-4218-2441-8

1st World Library is a literary, educational organization
dedicated to:

- Creating a free internet library of downloadable ebooks

- Hosting writing competitions and offering book
  publishing scholarships.

Interested in more 1st World Library books?
contact: literacy@1stworldlibrary.com
Check us out at: www.1stworldlibrary.com

1st World Library Literary Society

Giving Back to the World

"If you want to work on the core problem, it's early school literacy."

- James Barksdale, former CEO of Netscape

"No skill is more crucial to the future of a child, or to a democratic and prosperous society, than literacy."

- Los Angeles Times

Literacy... means far more than learning how to read and write... The aim is to transmit... knowledge and promote social participation."

- UNESCO

"Literacy is not a luxury, it is a right and a responsibility. If our world is to meet the challenges of the twenty-first century we must harness the energy and creativity of all our citizens."

- President Bill Clinton

"Parents should be encouraged to read to their children, and teachers should be equipped with all available techniques for teaching literacy, so the varying needs and capacities of individual kids can be taken into account."

- Hugh Mackay

CONTENTS

CHAPTER I

THE DIMPLESMITHY

Grown people have such an exasperating way of saying, "Now, when I was a little girl -"

Then, just as you prick up the little white ears of your mind for a story, they finish, loftily, "I did - or didn't do - so-and-so."

It is certainly an underhand way of suggesting that you stop doing something pleasant, or begin doing something unpleasant; and you would not have thought that Sara's dear mother would have had so unworthy a habit. But a stern regard for the truth compels me to admit that she had.

You see, Sara's dear mother was, indeed, most dear; but very self-willed and contrary. Her great fault was that she was always busy at something. She would darn, and she would write, and she would read dark-colored books without pictures. When Sara compared her with other mothers of her acquaintance, or when this very contrary own-mother went away for a day, she seemed indeed to Sara quite desperately perfect. But on ordinary days Sara was darkly aware, in the clearest part of her mind - the upper right-hand corner near the window - that her mother, with all her charm, really did need to be remoulded nearer to her heart's desire.

She was especially clear about this on the frequent occasions when she would come into the room where her mother was sitting, and plump down upon a chair with a heart-rending sigh, and say, "I wish I had somebody to play with!"

For then her dear but most contrary mother would glance up from her book or her darning and remark, with a calm smile,

"When I was a little girl -"

"Ah!"

"I used to go inside my head and play."

And Sara would answer with a poor, vindictive satisfaction, "There's nothing in my head to play with!"

And her kind-hearted mother would snip off her thread and say gently, in a tone of polite regret, "Poor little girl!"

Then Sara would gnash the little milk-teeth of her mind and have awful thoughts. The worst she ever had came one day when Mother, who had already filled about fourteen pages of paper with nothing in the world but words, acted that way again. And just as she said, "Poor little girl!" Sara thought, "I'd like to take that sharp green pencil and stick it into Mother's forehead, and watch a story run out of her head through the hole!"

But that was such an awful thought that she sent it scurrying away, as fast as she could. Just the same, she said to herself, if Mother ever acted that way again -

And, after all, Mother did. And that was the fatal time - the four-thousand-and-fourth. For, after Mother had suggested it four thousand and four times, it suddenly occurred to Sara that she might try it.

So she shut the doors and went in.

Yes, I said shut the doors and went in; for that is what you do when you go into your head. The doors were of ivory, draped with tinted damask curtains which were trimmed with black silk fringe. The curtains fell noiselessly behind Sara as she entered.

And there in the Gugollaph-tree by the pool sat the Plynck, gazing happily at her Echo in the water.

She was larger than most Plyncks; about the size of a small peacock. Of course you would know without being told that her plumage was of a delicate rose color, except for the lyre-shaped tuft on the top of her head, which was of the exact color and texture of Bavarian cream. Her beak and feet were golden, and her eyes were golden, too, and very bright and wild. The wildness and brightness of her eyes would have been rather frightening, if her voice, when she spoke, had not been so soft and sweet.

"I think a little girl has forgotten something," she said gently, looking down into her Teacup.

Sara examined herself anxiously. She knew it was something about herself, because the Plynck's tone was exactly like Mother's when she wished to remind Sara, without seeming officious, that she had not wiped her feet on the mat, or spread out her napkin, or remembered to say "Thank you" at the exact psychological moment.

Sara was extremely anxious to please the Plynck, because she thought her so pensive and pretty; but, try as she would, she couldn't think what she had forgotten to do.

"Does a little girl wear her dimples in The House?" asked the Plynck, still more gently.

"Oh, of course not!" said Sara, taking them off hastily. But she could not help adding, as she looked around appreciatively at the silver bushes and the blue plush grass and the alabaster moon-dial by the fountain, "But this isn't The House, is it?"

"Isn't it?" asked the Plynck, glancing uneasily about her. What she saw startled her so much that she dropped her Teacup. Of course it flew up to a higher branch and balanced itself there instead of falling; but the poor little thing was so round and fat, that - especially as it hadn't any feet - it had some difficulty at first in perching. As for the Plynck, she seemed so embarrassed over her mistake that Sara felt dreadfully uncomfortable for her. Recovering herself, however, in a moment, she said in her sweet, gentle way,

"Well, dear, you wouldn't want the Zizzes to fall into them, even if this isn't The House - would you?"

Sara hadn't noticed until then that the air was full of Zizzes; but the minute she saw their darling little vibrating wings she knew that she wouldn't for anything have one of them come to grief in her dimples. They were more like hummingbirds than anything she had ever seen outside of her head, but of course they were not nearly so large; most of them were about a millionth-part as large as a small mosquito. She noticed, too, that their tails were bitter. If it had not been for the bitterness of their tails, she would not have felt so uneasy about them; as it was, she held the dimples tight in her hand, with the concave side next her palm.

"Avrillia's at home," said the Plynck gently, with her eyes on her Teacup, which she was gradually charming back into her hand. (Her hands were feet, you know, like a nightingale's, only golden; but she called them hands in the afternoon, to match her Teacup.) The timid little thing was fluttering back, coming nearer twig by twig; and it trembled up to the Plynck just as she said, softly and absent-mindedly, "Avrillia's at home."

"Oh, is she?" exclaimed Sara, clapping her hands with joy. She did not know who Avrillia was; nevertheless, it somehow seemed delightful to hear that she was at home. But alas and

Karle Wilson Baker

alas! when she clapped her hands she forgot all about the dimples she had been holding so carefully. To tell the truth, she had never taken them off before; but she was ashamed to let the Plynck know about that, especially as she had lived in The House all her former life. Her first thought, indeed, when she realized what had happened, was to conceal the catastrophe from the Plynck; but before she could get her breath that gentle bird startled her almost out of her wits by shrieking,

"Watch out! the Snimmy will get it!"

And there, at Sara's feet, where a bit of the dimple lay on the taffy (looking very much like a fragile bit of a Christmas-tree ornament), was a real Snimmy, vest-pocket and all. His tail was longer than that of most Snimmies, and his nose was sharper and more debilitating, but you would have known him at once, as Sara did, for a Snimmy. She thought, too, that he trembled more than most of them, and that he was whiter and more slippery. Ordinarily, she had never felt afraid of Snimmies; but the startling shriek of the Plynck, and the exposed position of her dimple, set her to jumping wildly up and down. And, indeed, the worst would have happened, had not the Echo of the Plynck, with great presence of mind, cried out', "Cover it! Cover it!" And at that cry the Teacup fluttered hastily down and turned itself upside down over the piece of dimple. And there it sat, panting a little, but looking as plump and pleased as possible, though the Snimmy was still dancing and sniffing ferociously around its rim.

"There!" said the Plynck in her own gentle voice, though it still shook with excitement. "It's a mercy you settled without breaking." Then, turning to Sara, "And goodness knows how we'll ever get it out, Sara. It will take at least three onions to anaesthetize the Snimmy."

Now, this was indeed dreadful. Sara had been conscious enough before this announcement of the havoc she had wrought by her carelessness; and now to have brought down upon herself a word like that! She was almost ready to cry; and to keep from being quite ready, she suggested, tremulously, "Do you suppose I could go after the onions?"

The Plynck looked at her in surprise. "Why, didn't you bring them with you?" she said. Then, suddenly, she noticed how threateningly the Snimmy was dancing and squeaking around Sara's feet, and how Sara was shrinking away from him.

"He won't hurt you," she began. "He's perfectly kind and harmless, aside from his mania for dimples. He still smells the piece under the Teacup." Then, all at once, she grew rigid, and her golden eyes began to leap up and down like frightened flames.

"It's the ones in your hand!" she shrieked. "In your hand! Sit down for your life!"

Sara at first thought she had said, "Run for your life," and had indeed taken two-elevenths of a step; but when she realized that the Plynck had said, "Sit down for your life," she sat down precisely where she was, as if Jimmy had pulled a chair out from under her, on the very ice-cream brick her feet stood on. She realized that in a crisis like this obedience was the only safe thing. And the instant she touched the pavement, the Snimmy gave a great gulping sob and hid his face in his hands; and small, grainy tears the size of gum-drops began to trickle through them and fall into his vest-pocket.

The Echo of the Plynck in the water gave a rippling laugh of relief. "Well," she said, "it's a mercy you remembered that. Perhaps you don't know, my dear," she said, turning to Sara, "that no Snimmy can endure to see a mortal sit down. It simply breaks their hearts. See, he's even forgotten about the dimples."

And indeed, the Snimmy was standing before her, overcome by remorse. He was holding his shoe in his hand in the most gentlemanly manner, and Sara forgave him at once when she saw how sorry and ashamed he was.

Karle Wilson Baker

"I - hope you'll try to - to - to excuse me, Miss," he sobbed, humbly offering her a handful of gum-drops. "Them dimples - " here, for a moment, his nose began to wink and his feet pranced a little, but he looked closely to see that she was still sitting down, and controlled himself. "Them dimples -" he began again; but he could say no more. The gum-drops began falling all around like hail-stones, so fast that Sara felt that she ought to help him all she could - without getting up - to get them into his vest-pocket.

The clatter of the gum-drops again attracted the attention of the Plynck's Echo, who said, kindly, "Go and take a nap, now, Snimmy, and you'll feel better."

The Snimmy lifted his shoe and tried to reply, but he only gave a respectful sob. So he turned away and crept back to his home in the prose-bush - where, all this time, his wife had been sitting in plain sight on her own toadstool, grimly hemming the doorknob. At her feet lay her faithful Snoodle.

Up to this time, Sara had not ventured to address the Teacup. But, as she looked around and saw her still sitting there, so pleasant and bland and fragile, and with such a consanguineous handle, she felt a sudden certainty that the Teacup would always be kind and helpful; so she suggested timidly,

"Then we shan't need the onions?"

"Oh, dear, yes," answered the Teacup, in a soft, wrinkled voice. "We'd never in Zeelup be able to get the pieces of the dimple to Schlorge without first anaesthetizing the Snimmy."

Sara jumpled: that awful word again! Her head reeled (exactly as heads do in grown-up stories) as she realized how many things there were in this strange place that she didn't know. Who was Schlorge, for example? And how was she to get anything to anybody without getting up? And "anaesthetize"?

She hated to disturb the Teacup; she was knitting so placidly, and murmuring over and over to herself, "Never in Zeelup." She looked up into the tree; the Plynck, too, had fallen asleep, worn out by the unwonted excitement of the morning; and her lovely Echo also slept in the amber pool. Sara now noticed that, though the Plynck was rose-colored, her Echo was cerulean.

The great, soft, curled plumes of the Plynck and her Echo rippled as they breathed and slept, rather like water or fire in a little wind; and with every ripple they seemed to shake out a faint perfume that drifted across Sara's face in waves. And they both looked so lovely that she could not think of disturbing them, either. So she looked about to see if there might be any one else who could enlighten her.

And there at her elbow, as luck would have it, stood a Koopf. Up to this time, Sara had not been able to tell a Koopf from a Gunkus. To be sure, there isn't any difference, really; but you would think that any fairly imaginative child ought to be able to tell one. However, Sara now saw that the ground was swarming with Gunki.

"Do you know who Schlorge is?" asked Sara, rather timidly.

At first the Koopf only grinned. "Guess I do," he managed to say at last. Then he surprised and rather startled her by winking his left ear at her. "He's the best dimplesmith ever," he said at last. "He's - he's -" he began looking all about him, vaguely and a little wildly. But, just as Sara was growing a little afraid of him, his attention suddenly came back to her with a kind, businesslike interest. "Need some repairs?" he asked. "Some fractured dimples, maybe?"

"Yes, sir," said Sara, earnestly. "I have most of them here in my hand." She opened her hand and showed him the pretty little pieces.

"Where's the rest?" he inquired, with another grin. "Your plump friend, here, sitting on 'em?"

Karle Wilson Baker

Sara nodded.

The Koopf stooped and picked up one of the gum-drops that had rolled out of the Snimmy's vest-pocket. "Thought so," he said. "Happens every now and then. Only lately there ain't been anybody here that was dimpliferous, to speak of."

Then, suddenly, as if somebody had told him his house was on fire, he turned and set off down the path as fast as he could run. "Bring 'em to the shop!" he shouted back over his shoulder, excitedly. "Bring 'em to the shop!"

While Sara was looking after him, and wondering where the shop might be, and whether she dared try to get up without waking the Snimmy, the Koopf suddenly stopped running, and started thoughtfully back up the path toward her. "Don't know how I happened to forget it," he said, "but I - well, fact is, I'm - where's a stump? Where's a stump?" He looked hastily about him, and this time, seeing a stump near by, he clambered upon it, thrust one hand into his bosom and the other behind his back, like the pictures of Napoleon, and repeated, solemnly,

"I am Schlorge the Koopf, King of Dimplesmiths.

"Under the gright Gugollaph-tree
The Dimplesmithy stands;
The smith is harder than the sea
And softer than the lands;
He mends cheek-dimples frank and free,
But will not work on hands."

And as soon as he had finished he started wildly down the path again, shouting back, "Bring 'em to the shop!"

Sara sat looking down the path, then at the dimples in her hand. "Well," she said aloud, "I'm glad they're cheek-dimples, anyhow. But what in the world shall I do about the onions?"

"What in Zeelup," corrected the Teacup gently, counting her stitches. "Milder than swearing, my dear, more becoming, and quite as effective."

Sara wanted to tell her she wasn't swearing, but just at that moment the wife of the Snimmy remarked, with some disgust in her voice,

"Well, if you'd of asked me sooner, I could of told you. I have them in the sugar-bowl, of course. Do you suppose I'd be without, and him subject to such fits?"

And so saying, she replaced the doorknob, which was now neatly hemmed, on the front door of the prose-bush, and came down the steps to Sara, carrying three large onions. She was not a bad-looking person, though an amnicolist.

She then proceeded to slice the onions very deftly with a tuning-fork, after which she rubbed the ice-cream of the pavement with the slices, making a circle all around the Teacup, and another all around Sara, somewhat like the ring they used to burn about a fire in the grass, to keep it from spreading. All this time she was talking to them grumblingly, though she never once looked up.

"I should think anybody'd know better than to bring dimples around where he is," she said, "and I have my opinion of such. A poor, hardworking man like him, that tries to act moral. I should think -"

She kept on saying things like this, that made Sara feel very uncomfortable. But at last she finished her work, and looking watchfully back over her shoulder at the sleeping Snimmy, she said grudgingly to them both, "Now get up careful."

Sara rose to her feet, and the Teacup lifted her dainty little skirt ever so slightly. The minute the perfume from the dimples reached the Snimmy (he couldn't smell those in Sara's hand, of course, so long as she was sitting down), he sprang to

　　　　Karle Wilson Baker

his feet, quivering; but almost immediately he caught a whiff of the onions, and sank down again, entirely overcome, into a deep sleep.

The Teacup arose and shook out her skirts. She picked up the tiny, sparkling piece of dimple she had been protecting so long, and handed it prettily to Sara. "Now, my dear," she said, "I think I shall return to my mistress. I would suggest that you take your dimples to the shop immediately." So saying, she hopped up into the tree and settled quietly down beside the dreaming Plynck, taking great care not to disturb her. And Sara started down the path toward the Dimplesmithy.

The path turned presently into a wide road, very pleasant and peaceful-looking, and so deep with pollen-dust that Sara's shoes soon looked as if they were powdered with gold. Sunset sheep came wandering down the road now and then, and lines of white geese, and once she passed a little pond where green ducks were quacking and paddling; the road was so pretty, indeed, that it was hard for her to keep her mind on finding the Dimplesmithy. There were tall Gugollaph-trees all along the road, here and there, but Sara felt sure she would know the right one when she saw it. And sure enough, there it was, with the smithy in the shade of it, and the Koopf blowing up the fire in his forge with a pair of puff-ball bellows. She knew now why he had hurried home so fast: it was to put on his apron. It was of the finest mouse-hide, and he was plainly very proud of it.

He took the dimples from Sara at once, and showed a keen professional interest in them. He assured her that he had never seen a finer pair. "But you must take better care of them," he said.

He seemed so kind and interested that Sara thought perhaps he would help her with a problem she had been revolving in her mind ever since the accident. (She had fastened the problem on a little stick with a pin, like the paper windmills Jimmy made, so that she could turn it around very easily, and so see all sides of it.) So she asked the Koopf, quite respectfully,

"What ought I to do with them, when I shut the doors and come in?"

"Well," said the Koopf, judiciously, "the Plynck's Echo should have seen to that, first thing. Ought to have had a dimple-holder at the gate. Ought to know the Snimmy, by this time. A good fellow - can't help his failing. We used to keep a dimple-holder there all the time, but it's been so long, as I told you, since we've had anybody come along that was dimpliferous, to speak of. We've got sort of careless, I guess. I've got a very nice stock, here; I'll put one up before you go, so you'll know where to find it next time." As he spoke he took down from a shelf behind him a sort of receptacle which looked rather like a soap-bubble, rather like a gazing-globe; except that it had a tiny opening at the top, and a cushion of whipped cream in the bottom. Then he picked up from his bench the dimples, which he had been mending as he talked.

"It's a good thing the Snimmy can't see 'em now," he said, holding them off at arm's length and looking at them with frank admiration. "They're as good as new. Now let me show you what to do with 'em next time you come."

So saying, he dropped them into the holder, where they looked very pretty sparkling on the whipped cream cushion.

"Now," he said, "you carry them, and I'll bring the pedestal."

He tucked the pedestal under his arm, and they started back down the road together. It was very lovely to be trudging along under the late clear sky, through the sweet-smelling pollen-dust, and now and then meeting the sunset sheep, who, by this time, had found their little lambs. When they got back to the Garden, and stood in front of the gate through which Sara had entered, Schlorge had Sara sit down at once. It was really an unnecessary precaution, he said, since the holder was a non-conductor of dimple-waves, and not even the Snimmy could

Karle Wilson Baker

detect their presence when they were inside of it. "Still," said Schlorge, "I'll feel safer about 'em when they're on the pedestal out of his reach," and with that he took the globe from Sara's hands and fastened it deftly on the pedestal. Sara had never enjoyed herself more than she did as she sat by the amber waters in the fading light, watching the kind, clumsy Koopf (who was yet so skilful at his own work) place the pretty globe with so much pride and pleasure. She kept sniffing, meanwhile, at the tantalizing perfume that seemed to sift downward from the feathers of the Plynck, as she stirred, ever so softly, in her dreams.

At last the Koopf took a large slice of onion, which the Snimmy's wife had left convenient, and rubbed it all around the base of the pedestal.

"Now," he said, "if you'll always remember to stand inside of that circle, when you take 'em off and put 'em on, there won't be any more trouble. And take 'em off as soon as you shut the doors. If you dilly-dally a minute -"

At that moment the Plynck awoke and saw Sara. She stretched her warm, shimmering feathers and smiled.

"Avrillia's at home," she said, gently.

CHAPTER II

AVRILLIA

"I make it a rule," the Plynck was saying, as Sara dropped the curtain behind her the next morning, "to fly around the fountain at least twice every day." As she spoke, she reached out and took, from a bundle that lay within easy reach in a crotch of the Gugollaph-tree, something that looked like a little ivory stick. She snapped it easily with one golden claw, dropped the fragments, and reached out with careless grace for another.

"Oh," breathed Sara, clasping her hands. And she could not help adding, shyly, "If I could only see you when you fly - Madame Plynck!"

Sara was very proud of herself after she had said that. She had never called anybody "Madame" before, but she had read it in books, and it seemed just the title for a creature so beautiful and gentle and stately as the Plynck. It seemed so suitable that it gave her courage to repeat, "If I could only see you fly!"

"But I don't do it often, you see," answered the Plynck, quietly.

"Why - !" exclaimed Sara. "I thought you just said - " Not for worlds would she have seemed rude or impolite to the Plynck, but she was completely puzzled.

Karle Wilson Baker

The Plynck looked very kind. "I said I make it a rule," she said, gently. "I didn't say - you explain it to her," she said suddenly to her Echo in the pool, who had been looking on with rather an amused expression.

The Echo fluffed out her deep blue plumes a little and took up the task. "What are rules for, my dear?" she began.

"Why - to keep, I guess," ventured Sara, a little flustered. "Aren't they?"

The Echo glanced up at the Plynck with a twinkling smile. "Do you hear that?" she asked. "Bless the child! She says rules are made to keep!" She laughed to herself a little longer, then she turned to Sara more soberly. "As far as your country is concerned, my dear, you are doubtless right, and I suppose it's important for you to keep that fact in mind. But here it's very different. Our rules are made to break. Don't you hear the Plynck breaking them?"

So that was what she was doing! For the first time, Sara understood why she had so enjoyed the delightful little snapping sounds, which made her think of corn dancing against the lid of a corn-popper - or of the snapping of little dry twigs under the pointed shoes of a brownie, slipping through the woods alone on Christmas Eve. She thought it was the most completely satisfying sound she had ever heard. She thought, too, that the broken rules under the tree made a charming litter, and wished that the Gunki who were raking them up would leave them there instead. But they went on piling them into wheelbarrows and trundling them down the road toward the smithy.

"They are taking them to be mended," said the Echo of the Plynck, who had been watching her. "We believe in conservation, you see. Schlorge mends them one day, and she breaks them the next, and so we usually have plenty."

Sara was charmed. But as she stood gazing at the Plynck she

remembered what she had heard her say as she came in. "Will - will she fly?" she whispered to the Echo.

"Well, I don't know," said the Echo of the Plynck. "There's a rule that she must, and so it's quite an effort. And there's a rule that she must not sit on that particular branch of the Gugollaph-tree. So of course she usually sits there. You wouldn't think, yourself, that she'd want to sit there, day after day, if there wasn't - would you?"

Sara was speechless; she was wondering why anything that seemed so reasonable and familiar should sound so strange. But it was a blissful wonder, and she stood spellbound, while the sound of breaking rules continued to fall with an enchanting effect upon the still air of the Garden. All at once she was startled nearly out of her wits by the Plynck, who dropped an unbroken rule and shrieked,

"Look! Be careful! Oh, dear, oh, dear, it's in!"

"Oh, what is it?" cried Sara, afraid to move, yet longing to clap her hand to her cheek; for she knew by a sudden terrible tickling there that something had happened to her southwest dimple - and she had meant to be so careful! And yet she had allowed herself to get so interested in the talk of the Plynck and her Echo that she had walked right past Schlorge's beautiful dimple-holder. "What is it?" she cried, jumping up and down. "Oh, what is it?"

"It's one of the Zizzes!" cried the Plynck. "Where are the forceps? Run for Schlorge - won't somebody please run for Schlorge?"

She sat fluttering her lovely pink plumes and gazing around with her sweet, wild, golden eyes in such acute distress that the sight of her grieved and terrified Sara even more than the awful tickling. "I'll go - " she began, desperately.

But that seemed to frighten the Plynck more than ever. "Oh,

don't you go," she cried, more wildly than before. "You stay right here where I can watch it! Oh, somebody - "

"I can't come out of the pool," panted her Echo, fluttering around the rim distressfully.

"I know I could never in Zeelup get there, with this consanguineous handle," hesitated the Teacup, in tears.

And just then they saw one of the Gunki rushing off down the road as fast as his feet could carry him.

The Plynck drew a sobbing breath of relief. "Don't cry, dear - stand still," she said, finding time at last to feel sorry for Sara. "We'll soon have it out now, when Schlorge gets here."

Sara stood as still as she could, for the tickling. "What is it?" she ventured to ask, tremulously.

"It's a Zizz, dear," said the Plynck, soothingly. "He flew into your dimple and got stuck in the sugar left there from your last smile. You should have wiped it off," she added, very gently. "Standing so close to the pool has made it sticky, and now the poor little Zizz -"

"I meant to take off my dimples entirely," said Sara, her lip beginning to tremble again.

"Never mind, dear," said the Plynck. "It will be all right now. I see Schlorge coming with his forceps."

And sure enough, in a moment Schlorge came panting up, with his forceps in his hair, as usual. Very deftly he extricated the poor little Zizz, and held it out for Sara to see, still buzzing its wings as furiously as it could, with so much syrup on them.

The Teacup fluttered down, and they all looked at it with mingled sympathy and curiosity. The mixture seemed to agree with it, too, for the familiar faint, pale-blue "zizzing" sound began to come from its wings.

"Poor little thing!" said the Echo of the Plynck. "Why will they persist in doing it? Flying right into the syrup like that!"

"It's on account of the bitterness of their tails," explained Schlorge absently, without looking up from his work.

"Oh, yes," said Sara, though she didn't quite understand. "Will it ever be able to fly again?"

"Well," answered Schlorge, "I'm afraid you'll have to dry it." He looked about him. "Where's the stump?"

He found it presently, and led Sara to its mossy base; then he gently pressed one of her shoe-buttons, and she was lifted upon it in safety.

"Now," he explained, "you got it all sticky with your smile, and you'll have to frown on it to dry it. I know it's hard to do, here, but if you keep your mind on it, you can. I'll hold the Zizz's wings out, and it won't take long. Think of something very unpleasant - something you came here to escape. Come, what shall it be?"

"Fractions," said Sara.

"All right," said Schlorge. "Now think hard. And frown."

So Sara sucked in the corners of her mouth to keep from smiling, and tried hard to feel very cross indeed. But, as you will imagine, it was not easy to do in that place. As you have already guessed, the place into which Sara went when she shut the ivory doors was a sort of garden, but not an ordinary one. To be sure, it had the pool, and the fountain in the middle, and the moon-dial, like most gardens, and the Gugollaph-tree where the Plynck sat, and a good many prose-bushes besides the one with the hemmed doorknob where the Snimmy lived with his wife. But not many gardens have such charming little

Karle Wilson Baker

openings in the flowery hedges that shut them in, through which little paths run out as if they were escaping through sheer mischief, and on purpose to lead you on. And not many are placed, as this one seemed to be, in the middle of a sort of amphitheatre, with distant mountains rising like walls about it, golden and pansy-colored, a million miles away. The space that lay between the hedge and the mountain-walls seemed to be filled with sunrises and sunsets, like the Grand Canyon. I said, all around; but, really, the walls of the amphitheatre didn't quite meet. On one side, over the hedge, Sara could see a marble balcony, with box-trees in vases on the balustrades; and beyond and beneath it there was Nothing - Nothing-at-All. Sometimes, as Sara afterward learned, the sun came to that place to set; but usually it was too lonesome, and he set nearer the Garden.

You may well imagine that it was not easy for Sara to look cross in such a strange, delicious place. But she knew she owed it to the poor little Zizz, so she tried with all her might to think only of fractions and asparagus. (Her mother had an obstinate conviction that that, too, was good for children.)

They were all so interested in listening to the deepening blueness of the sound the Zizz made that they kept quite still. Suddenly Schlorge thought of something.

"Where's the Snimmy?" he asked, sharply.

"He's gone with his wife to bathe the Snoodle," answered the Echo of the Plynck. "They have to bathe it every three days, you know, in castor oil. That's what keeps it white. And there isn't any here."

"Thank goodness!" thought Sara, who had nearly jumped off the stump at the sound of those baleful syllables. It would be good to think of, anyhow, she decided; and as she thought of it, the wings of the Zizz began to dry so fast that they fairly sang. And suddenly it zizzed right out of Schlorge's forceps and went buzzing straight off to the flowery hedge.

"Well!" said Schlorge, with much satisfaction, "that's over." Then, as Sara's face twinkled into smiles, he added, excitedly, "Bless my bellows! She's still got on her dimples! Won't you learn, Sara? Course I didn't notice 'em while you frowned. Come, now -"

"And it's time for the Snimmy to be back," interrupted the Teacup, who had fluttered down and perched on the edge of the moon-dial to see what time it was. "They said they'd only be gone two hours."

"Then there's no time to lose," said Schlorge. He pressed Sara's shoe-button decidedly and she floated softly down upon the blue plush, like a milk-weed seed in the fall. And then Schlorge deftly took off her dimples - it felt very funny to have them removed with the forceps - and put them in the dimple-holder where they belonged. Then, drawing a deep breath, he rubbed his hands and smiled at her, saying, "What's the next thing you'd like to do?"

Sara saw that, though he was still rather bashful, Schlorge had taken a great fancy to her. It pleased her very much; he was such a useful and accommodating person. While she was trying to decide which one of several places she would ask him to show to her, the Plynck remarked, gently,

"Avrillia's at home."

Avrillia - that was it! Sara clapped her hands again, and this time no harm was done; for her cheek-dimples were safe in the dimple-holder, and her hand-dimples were on the outside, so that the clapping only jarred them a little. It was funny, she thought, that Schlorge scorned to work on hand-dimples, and even the Snimmy scarcely noticed them. But it didn't worry her. Avrillia - that was it. She had come this time especially to see Avrillia.

"Do you know where she lives?" she asked Schlorge.

"Avrillia? I should say so. Everybody knows Avrillia. At least I know her to speak to. As to what goes on inside of her, I can't say. She's queer. She writes poetry, you know."

"But she's nice?" asked Sara anxiously.

"Oh, she's pleasant-spoken," said Schlorge, "and pretty. Some like her, and some don't. The Plynck, here," he spoke respectfully, though dissentingly, "thinks the sun rises and sets in her. For myself, I like folks of a more sensible turn."

"Even fairies?" asked Sara, half inclined to protest.

For the first time Schlorge was almost rude to her. "Well, do you take me for a human? And I can do something besides write poetry on rose-leaves." He replaced the forceps in his hair with obvious professional pride - and, of course, when he put them in in that way, they stayed.

But Sara echoed delightedly, "On rose-leaves?"

"Well, go and see her, then," said Schlorge, ungraciously. Then, relenting a little, "Come on, I'll take you - if you're stuck on verse-writing females."

He took Sara by the hand, and of course his hand was kinder than his voice. To Sara's joy they struck into the curliest of the little paths, which slipped suddenly through a half-hidden arch in the hawthorn hedge, and then skipped confidingly right up to Avrillia's door. Avrillia's house was right on the Verge, but the Verge was quite wide at this point, and very lovely. It was more like a beach than anything else; and the sands, of course, like those of most beaches, were of gold; but instead of being bare, like most beaches, it was sprinkled quite thickly with lovely clumps of fog-bushes, which were of a different color every hour of the day and every day of the year; and the shells had stems and leaves, and were prettier even than most shells. And Avrillia's house had sails, instead of curtains. Still, it was not a boat, because it had star-vines climbing all over the terrace (the flowers were of all colors, except square, and only opened in the evening) and it had the marble balcony, with the box-trees in urns. For, without knowing it, it was Avrillia's balcony that Sara had seen from the stump.

"Well, there's Pirlaps," said Schlorge, lifting his shoe politely and turning back toward the Dimplesmithy. "He'll tell you where to find Avrillia."

Sara was left looking at a middle-aged fairy-gentleman with a little pointed beard, who was sitting on a sort of stool or box before an easel, hard at work. He had on white tennis-flannels, and an odd but becoming sort of cap. Usually Sara was very shy of strangers; but this gentleman looked so pleasant that she had almost made up her mind to speak to him when she saw Schlorge running wildly back up the path. "Where's a stump?" he panted. "I forgot - where's a stump?"

He spoke so loudly that the gentleman in tennis-flannels heard him and looked around. "Oh, it's you, Schlorge," he said. "Why, there isn't any stump here, you know - but you may use my step, if you like."

He had lovely manners, even with a plain dimplesmith like Schlorge; and he rose as he spoke, with his palette in his hand, and made a pleasant gesture to indicate that Schlorge was quite welcome to it. But Schlorge looked at it doubtfully; and, indeed, Sara saw that it was of chocolate, and rather soft where the gentleman had been sitting on it. "I don't want to soil my soul," mumbled Schlorge, standing on one foot and looking down at the sole of the other, very much agitated and embarrassed.

"That's true," said the gentleman politely; "I never stand on it." At that Sara could not help showing that she noticed the large black spot left by the chocolate on the seat of his trousers. He saw her look at it, and spoke to her kindly.

"That's all right, little girl," he said. "Avrillia will have me change them in a minute."

Then he noticed Schlorge's dreadful impatience for something to stand on, and rang a little bell in his left ear.

Immediately a small servant, also of chocolate, came tumbling out of the house. He was the most attractive-looking person you can imagine. His eyes and teeth were exactly like the filling in a chocolate cream, and how his eyes rolled and his teeth twinkled! But it was the inside of his mouth that fascinated Sara most. It was of the lovely, violent red of certain jelly-beans she had known, and she caught the most tantalizing, cavernous glimpses whenever he grinned.

"Yassuh," said his master, "go at once and get a piece of plain white satin for Mr. Schlorge to stand on. You'll find a bolt in the tool-box."

Yassuh scrambled off down the path. (He was very bow-legged, because his mother had allowed him to go out in the sun too much, when he was a baby, and, being of chocolate, his legs had softened into that shape.) Almost immediately he came rolling back with the white satin, which he spread on the box.

All this time Schlorge had been in an agony of impatience. Almost stepping on Yassuh in his eagerness, he jumped upon the box, and, arranging his hands as before, shouted loudly, "Pirlaps, this is Sara, a little girl! Sara, this is Pirlaps, Avrillia's step-husband!" Then he sprang down and went running down the path again, shouting excitedly, "See you again, Sara! See you again!"

"Well, Sara," said the pleasant fairy-gentleman, taking her hand, "how are you? Did you come to see Avrillia?"

"Yes, sir," said Sara, looking up at him from under her lashes and thinking she had never see a shaving-person, except her own father, so delightful.

"I think you'll find her on her balcony," said Pirlaps, kindly. "I just heard a poem drop over the Verge. Here, Yassuh," he said, "take this little girl to your mistress."

Sara followed Yassuh along the path of silver gravel that led around the house, and then up a little outside staircase of marble to the balcony; and there, on the third step from the top, she paused.

Has any mortal but Sara ever seen Avrillia? Certainly there never was another fairy so wan and wild and beautiful. When Sara caught sight of her she was leaning over the marble balustrade, looking down into Nothing, and one hand was still stretched out as if it had just let something fall. She seemed to be still watching its descent. Her body, as she leaned, was like a reed, and her hair was pale-gold and cloudy. But all that was nothing beside Avrillia's eyes.

For she turned around after a while and saw Sara, and smiled at her without surprise, though she looked absent-minded and wistful.

"It didn't stick," she said.

"What didn't?" asked Sara. Her words may not sound very polite; but if you could have heard the awe and wonder in her little voice you would have pardoned her.

"The poem," said Avrillia. What was it her voice was like? Sheep-bells? Sheep-bells, that was it. Sheep-bells across an English down - at twilight! Sara had never seen more than three sheep in her life; and those three didn't wear bells; and she had never heard of a down. And yet, Avrillia's voice sounded to Sara exactly as I have said.

Moreover, it drew Sara softly to her side. Her dress smelled like isthagaria; and it was very soft to touch. For Sara touched it as confidingly as she would her own mother's.

Karle Wilson Baker

At that Avrillia seemed to remember her. Sara saw at once that Avrillia never remembered anybody very long at a time. She was kind, and her smile was entrancingly sweet; but her mind always seemed to be on something else. Probably on her poetry, Sara decided.

Now, however, she remembered Sara, and asked, "Would you like to look over?"

"What's down there?" Sara could not help asking.

"Nothing. Would you like to see it?"

Sara drew nearer the balustrade, full of awe, and uncertain whether she wished to look or not. But presently curiosity got the better of her, and she leaned over the balustrade and looked down into Nothing. It was very gray.

"Do you throw your poems down there?" she asked of Avrillia, in inexpressible wonder.

"Of course," said Avrillia. "I write them on rose-leaves, you know -"

"Oh, yes!" breathed Sara. She still thought she had never heard of anything that sounded lovelier than poems written on rose-leaves.

"Petals, I mean, of course," continued Avrillia, "all colors, but especially blue. And then I drop them over, and some day one of them may stick on the bottom -"

"But there isn't any bottom," said Sara, lifting eyes like black pansies for wonder.

"No, there's no real bottom," conceded Avrillia, patiently, "but there's an imaginary bottom. One might stick on that, you know. And then, with that to build to, if I drop them in very fast, I may be able to fill it up -"

"But there aren't any sides to it, either!" objected Sara, even more wonderingly.

Avrillia betrayed a faint exasperation (it showed a little around the edges, like a green petticoat under a black dress). "Oh, these literal people!" she said, half to herself. Then she continued, still more patiently, "Isn't it just as easy to imagine sides as a bottom? Well, as I was saying, if I write them fast enough to fill it up - I mean if one should stick, of course - somebody a hundred years from now may come along and notice one of my poems; and then I shall be Immortal." And at that a lovely smile crossed Avrillia's face.

Sara stood a long time, thinking. She couldn't help loving Avrillia, although she knew that Avrillia was not nearly so fond of her as the Plynck, or Schlorge, or even the Teacup. Yet she would have loved Avrillia, even if she had not been kind to her at all.

Now she attracted her attention again by timidly touching her dress.

"It - it seems a waste," she murmured. I think probably she was thinking of the rose-petals rather than of the poems. All those lovely "rose-leaves"! And she had never seen even one blue one. But Avrillia was thinking of the poems.

"That's the regular way to do about Poetry," she said, with a pretty little air of authority. "First, you write it, and then you drop it over the Verge into Nothing. But it must be very good - otherwise, it isn't worth while to spend your time on it." But just then the thermometer went off.

Yes, the thermometer. Well, perhaps you do set the alarm-clock; but Avrillia was a poetess, and a fairy besides, and she set the alarm-thermometer. It sounded very pleasant to Sara, like soda-water running through a straw on a hot afternoon; but Avrillia seemed to find it rather nerve-racking.

Karle Wilson Baker

"There it goes," was all she said, however. Sara noticed that her voice and manner were extremely quiet and controlled; but she had a suspicion that it was because her eyes were so very wild. Oh, yes, they were beautiful, but wild - wilder even than the Plynck's. The Teacup, however, had quite tame eyes; it must be confessed that, when Sara saw the effect of the thermometer upon Avrillia she wished for the Teacup, a little.

But Avrillia merely called Yassuh in her sweet, controlled voice, and, when he appeared, said to him quietly,

"Go tell your master it's time for him to change his trousers and shave."

When Yassuh was gone she turned to Sara again - rather as one entertains a visitor when one really wants to be doing something else - and said, politely, "I suppose you know he's my step-husband. That makes it rather troublesome."

Sara, remembering Pirlaps and his white trousers, looked so eager and so uncomprehending that Avrillia evidently felt called upon to explain further.

"It makes it necessary for him to sit on the step constantly, you see. And it's of chocolate. That's unfortunate, too, but it can't be helped. It's all right in winter, of course, but in summer it's a great deal of trouble. When we were first married he used to wear black trousers in summer; but I soon put a stop to that. I have him trained now so that he always wears white ones, and I set the thermometer and remind him to change them every two hours. That's my part of the bargain. He has forty-seven pairs. And, every time he changes them, he has to shave. That's part of the agreement, too."

"Why," began Sara, "I thought he had -"

"To be sure he has," said Avrillia, looking a little amused. "It grows so fast, you see."

Sara turned this over in her mind for several moments. Then her thoughts returned to the step. She simply couldn't help making suggestions to Avrillia. She seemed, for all her little haughty politenesses, so helpless.

"You might put something over it - " she began.

"I have suggested that," said Avrillia, "but he would not consent to it. He says it would be circumnavigating Nature. Of course, when it's necessary to offer it to guests - "

But just at that moment Pirlaps himself came out of the house, wearing a fresh, immaculate pair of trousers. His little pointed beard was gone; but Sara thought she could see it already coming back. Yassuh came along behind him, carrying the step.

"You see, marriage is very civilizing, Sara," he said, in his gay, kind way. "I wouldn't do this for anybody but Avrillia. How's the poetry, Avrillia?"

"Doing nicely, thank you," said Avrillia, pleasantly. "How's the painting?"

"Flourishing," said Pirlaps, cheerfully. "How are the children?"

"I haven't seen them this week," said Avrillia. "I vanished them last Roseday."

Pirlaps' face fell a little - perhaps an inch, altogether. But Sara cried out, clapping her hands again with impunity (try doing it that way, sometime - it's great fun),

"Oh, are there children?"

"Yes," said Avrillia.

"How many?"

"Oh, about seventy," said Avrillia, a little languidly.

"May - may I see them?" asked Sara.

"I hope so," said Avrillia. "Perhaps you'll come some day when they're not vanished."

Sara, somehow, felt herself to have been politely dismissed; and she soon found herself walking beside Pirlaps down the little marble stairs. She slipped her hand into his as she would into her own father's, and, looking up into his face, said, enthusiastically, "Oh, isn't she lovely?"

Pirlaps seemed very much pleased, and looked down upon her more kindly than ever. "You like Avrillia?" he said. "That's good. It isn't everybody that appreciates Avrillia."

He stopped before a lilac-colored fog-bush and put his step down before his easel. Sara did not dare remonstrate, but she cast an agonized look first at the step and then at his lovely white trousers.

"Is - is that what is meant by step-relations?" was all she could say.

"Why, yes," said Pirlaps, sitting firmly down on the chocolate. "Are you interested in relations?" he asked eagerly, after he had adjusted his easel. "Because, if you are, we'll go to see mine, some day. I have a lot."

CHAPTER III

RELATIONS

Sara was determined, when she shut the ivory doors behind her the next morning, to do two things, no matter what happened; first, she would put her dimples in the dimple-holder immediately; and, second, she would go right on to find Pirlaps, and not be beguiled into lingering around the pool by the fascinating talk of the Plynck and her Echo. For, ever since she left him, she had been thinking of the offer Pirlaps had made to take her to see his relations; and she had been growing more and more curious and interested.

And this time she did remember her dimples; she saw them sparkling on the whipped cream cushion, all safe and contented, before she so much as lifted her eyes from the blue plush grass. But alas, for her resolution not to loiter! For although, on the other days, there had been such a variegated murmur of delighted sound - the Echo of the Plynck in the pool, and the lovely crackling of breaking rules, and the deep-blue singing of the Zizzes' wings, and the melodious snoring of the Snoodle (like that of a tuning-fork when it sleeps on its side) - yet everything had been as still and motionless to the eye as an April daydream. But this morning it was the other way around. Not a sound was to be heard; but what a scene! You see, for the first time, the Snoodle was awake, frisking soundlessly around the fountain; and the Plynck - the Plynck was flying!

Karle Wilson Baker

Now, it is true that a Plynck at rest is a beautiful sight; but it is nothing to the charm and wonder of a Plynck in motion. (The same, as we shall see in a moment, is true in a lesser degree of a Snoodle.) Its long, rosy plumes, like those of an ostrich, only four times as long, went waving through the air with an indescribably dreamy grace; and now Sara could actually see the perfume, which before she had only smelled. It rained down through the air, as the Plynck circled slowly round and round the fountain, and looked rather like a sort of golden spice. And as Sara stood watching, spellbound and sniffing, she knew she had been mistaken in thinking that, there was no sound at all. There was just one: a little soft, straining sound the Plynck's cerulean Echo made as it circled round and round in the pool and tried to keep up with the Plynck. Her motions would have been exactly as lovely as those of the Plynck, if they had not been just a trifle labored, owing to the difficulty of flying under water; and her breathing was distinctly perceptible. Sara could hear it, too; and it sounded like the ghost of a dead breeze in a pine-top.

As soon as Sara could take her ravished eyes from the sight, she looked down to see what was nuzzling about her shoe-buttons; and, just as she had suspected, it was the Snoodle, frisking and tumbling and rolling about her feet to make her notice him. And, indeed, when he was awake, the Snoodle was irresistible. Not that he looked like anything Sara had ever seen before. He might, perhaps, have looked like a dog, except that he was so very long - his length, indeed, gave him a haunting resemblance to a freshly cooked piece of macaroni. (Sara was later to find out the reason for this; but at the moment she was puzzled, just as you are when you meet a stranger who looks like somebody else, and you can't remember who else it is.) And his head, which was not very clearly defined, was finished off with a neat little cap that looked like a snail-shell, and seemed to be fastened to him. His eyes, which stuck out several inches in front of his face on long prongs, were delightfully mischievous and confiding; and he was covered with the most beautiful snow-white, curly hair. But he had one drawback; and Sara discovered that when she started to pick him up. It was a sort of little window in the exact middle of his back, with an ising-glass cover, like the slide-cover of some boxes. The minute you touched him, this little slide drew back, and from within there escaped an odor of castor oil. It, too, was distinctly perceptible; Sara could even smell it. As soon as she did so, she herself drew back, and contented herself with looking admiringly at the confiding, playful little Snoodle.

As she stood watching his pretty antics she became aware that the Snimmy's wife had stopped her work and was watching them with a grim smile. Sara saw that she had just unscrewed the knob of the prose-bush, and was still holding the doorknob and the corkscrew in her hand. As far as Sara could tell, the doorknob seemed as neatly hemmed as ever; so, overcome by curiosity, she asked the Snimmy's wife what she was going to do with it.

"This is the day to unhem it," she answered rather glumly. "I unhem it every Pinkday, and hem it every Lilyday. I used to hem it only oncet a month, but Avrillia said that wasn't civilized, and whatever she says, goes. At least," she added, glancing up at the Plynck, who was still circling beautifully around the fountain, "she thinks so. And as long as I live neighbor to her it's sort-of up to me to respect her standards."

Avrillia! Ah, now Sara remembered! She had meant to go straight to find Pirlaps and Avrillia! She glanced around to see if she could find the curly little path; but she could not really start until she had asked a few questions about the darling little Snoodle.

"Is - isn't he lovely?" she began, aware of a vague necessity of pleasing the wife of the Snimmy, if one wanted to find out anything. However, she was quite honest; she really did think the Snoodle was lovely - except for his drawback.

"You think so?" answered the Snimmy's wife, trying hard not to show how foolishly pleased she really was. "He's the only child we have."

If Sara had thought a minute, she would not have asked the next question - certainly not of so formidable a person as the Snimmy'swife. But she didn't think. She just asked, eagerly,

"Is he a - a sort of - dog?"

"A sort of *dog*?" echoed the Snimmy's wife, in the most outraged italics.

"A - kind of - puppy?"

"A kind of - PUPPY?" said the Snimmy's wife, in perfectly withering small capitals. Then she said, in the loftiest large capitals Sara had ever seen,

"HIS MOTHER WAS A SNAIL - SHE HELD THE WORLD'S RECORD FOR SLOWNESS. AND HIS FATHER WAS A PEDIGREED NOODLE."

Sara looked at him in awe; now she understood the cap, and the prongs, and the extreme length. But, in spite of the Snimmy's wife's indignant mood, she had to ask one more question.

"But you said he was your child," was the way she put it.

"I didn't," retorted the Snimmy's wife, with undisguised contempt. "I said he was the only child we have. We have him, haven't we?" And with that she sat down with her back to Sara on her own toadstool, and curled her long white tail around the base with quite unnecessary tightness. Her nose was not quite so debilitating as the Snimmy's; still, it nearly stuck into the doorknob as she hemmed.

Sara saw there was nothing further to be got out of her, and she did not wish to pick up the Snoodle on account of his drawback; so she decided to go on to Avrillia's without further delay, and began to look around her again for the little curly path. It was pink, this time, instead of curly, but that made it all the more attractive; so she struck into it at once, and went skipping happily toward the arch in the hawthorn hedge. Just before she reached it she heard Avrillia's thermometer go off, so she knew that she was on the right path.

The minute she got through the hedge she saw Avrillia, and, oh, loveliest of wonders! What were those? Flying around her hair, clinging to her silken skirts, dancing among the shell-flowers, swarming over the balcony, playing a dainty game up and down the marble stairs - oh, it was the children! The children were at home!

And when Avrillia saw Sara she came toward her with the loveliest look of welcome, the children hanging all around her like rose-garlands. And if Sara had loved Avrillia the day before, she could simply find no words now to express her adoration. For Avrillia knelt down among the shell-flowers, and held out her arms (which were like the necks of swans) to Sara; and she really seemed to see her this time. And when she smiled at her, her eyes were hardly at all wild, but quite playful and gentle; and so sweet that Sara, for a moment, had a dizzy conviction that if she were a Zizz she would fly right into them. (Though, of course, the Zizzes' tails were bitter.) Besides, Avrillia held her at that minute tight to her breast, which was as soft as her own perfect, contrary mother's, and had, besides a most entrancing, faint perfume of isthagaria.

When she had finished hugging Sara, she held her off at arms' length, and said to her, smiling, in that lovely voice,

"Well, Sara, you see the children are here. Aren't they nice?"

And once more Sara could find no words to express their niceness. And she could no more have described them to you than if they had been so many endearing young charms. But one of the queerest, prettiest things she was sure about: their faces were all dimples! Moreover, they were much more becoming to them than ordinary features would have been.

"How old are they?" asked Sara, in the most delighted bewilderment. The friendly little things fluttered and chattered and chirruped around her in the most distracting way, brushing her face with their wings in their eagerness to get acquainted, and even getting their silver sandals tangled in her hair.

"Well," said Avrillia with great exactitude - Sara had already discovered that Avrillia had a weakness for being considered practical - "fourteen of them are six and three of them are two and thirty are seven and ten are nine, and five are six months."

"My!" said Sara, in doubt and wonder. And right there she had a suspicion that that was one reason she had loved Avrillia from the first: she couldn't do arithmetic! To be sure, Sara herself couldn't add all that mixture in her head - at least not with all those lovely children about - but it sounded like a great deal more than seventy; and there certainly looked to be a million. So, as she stood and gazed, she said, more in wonder than with any idea of correcting Avrillia, "And you said there were just seventy?"

For a moment Avrillia's eyes again grew distraught and doubtful, and she answered, uncertainly, "I think there are just seventy." Then she called to Pirlaps, who was sitting on his step in the light of a glorious flame-colored fog-bush, hard at work, "Pirlaps, have we had any children since Sara was here yesterday?"

"Not one," said Pirlaps, smiling at her with a look of pleasant amusement. "Don't you remember that you dropped poems over the Verge all day?"

"I thought so," said Avrillia, with relief, "but Sara seemed to think there were more than seventy." Then her eyes fell upon the trousers of Pirlaps, who had risen and was coming toward them now, with Yassuh rolling along behind with the step.

"O Pirlaps," said Avrillia, her sweet voice full of reproach, "you haven't changed your trousers! That's just the way things go," she added, beginning to look wild and worried and distraught, "when the children are here! I can't keep up with everything! And the thermometer went off fifteen minutes ago! I heard it, but I was busy with the children. And your shaving-water will be perfectly cold!" She grew more and more agitated.

"Never mind, Avrillia," said Pirlaps, soothingly, and Sara noticed that his pleasant, cheerful ways always had a wonderfully calming effect upon Avrillia. "I'm going right in now to change; and then I have a plan that will straighten things out and please everybody."

"What is it?" asked Avrillia, looking more hopeful.

"It's too soon to tell yet," said Pirlaps, with a delightfully wise air, and he went on up the steps, with Yassuh tumbling after him, leaving them all feeling very much relieved.

Avrillia, making a brave effort to recover her composure, began playing with the children again, and they were having almost as delightful a time as if nothing distressing had occurred, when Pirlaps reappeared, all fresh-shaven and immaculate.

"Put the step out in the sun where it will keep soft, Yassuh," he said. "I shan't need it this afternoon."

They all stopped playing and looked at him in wonder.

"I'm going to take Sara to see my relations, as I promised her I would," he explained, taking Sara kindly by the hand.

"Oh, that's lovely," said Avrillia, looking at Pirlaps gratefully out of her speaking eyes. "There's nobody like you, Pirlaps."

Pirlaps looked wonderfully pleased with himself; and, since there was not a bit of chocolate on his trousers, he looked unusually spruce and handsome, too. Sara skipped along beside him delightedly; only, sometimes when she looked back, she wished she could stay with Avrillia while she was in such a lovely mood, and all those interesting children. Still, Sara's dear, self-willed mother had taught her to be a considerate little girl, and she reflected that she really ought not to bother Avrillia with another child, when she already had seventy to look after. The thoughts of Pirlaps also seemed to be running in the same channel (indeed, Sara could catch glimpses of them, trickling along under that thin, funny cap he always wore), and he presently said,

"It's too bad to bring you away when the children are at home, Sara, but you know they are a great deal of care to Avrillia, and when they're at home I try to do everything I can to relieve her. Now, you see, she won't have to bother about my trousers for the whole afternoon."

"But how can you get along without your step?" asked Sara. She knew this was a personal question, but she felt, somehow, that Pirlaps would not think her impolite.

He looked down at her and smiled, just as her own father did when she asked questions which showed her youth and inexperience.

"I'm not a step-man, Sara," he said, his eyes twinkling with amusement at her lack of information, "only a step-husband. When I'm away from Avrillia I don't need the step."

All this time they had been walking along hand in hand. Sara noticed that they had left the Verge behind, and were following a very pleasant sort of ridge, from which they could see down into a sort of hollow for smiles and smiles, and, beyond the hollow, the buff-colored hills and mountains that formed the walls of the amphitheatre. There were not so many Gugollaph-trees as there were in the Garden and along the road to the Dimplesmithy, owing to the different topography of the country; instead, there were a good many poker-bushes.

"My relations live in a colony," said Pirlaps. "There used to be nearly seven hundred of them; but now there are only eight hundred and three."

And just at that moment they came in sight of the colony. It consisted in a large number of odd, attractive-looking little houses grouped around an open space covered with pleasant red grass, which Pirlaps told her was an uncommon. In the middle of the uncommon was a sort of platform, and upon the platform there was something which Sara, at first glance, took to be an enormous statue. But even at that distance she could see it move; so she hastened to ask Pirlaps what it was.

"Why, that's my Great-Great-Great-Great-Grandfather," said Pirlaps, with a good deal of pride. "He occupies the Post of Honor in the colony, you know, because he's the oldest and the largest. He's really great, and quite pleasant; you'll enjoy meeting him."

By this time they were going down a little shady road that led straight to the uncommon. Sara was so struck by the large number of curious and interesting people she saw on all sides, going quietly about their regular occupations, that she could hardly look where she was going. But Pirlaps led her right to the foot of the post, and the first thing she knew he was introducing her. "This is Sara, Great-Great-Great-Great," he was saying; and Sara looked up and saw, sitting in a sort of easy chair on top of the post, the very largest person she had ever seen. In size he was a veritable giant, or even an ogre; but anybody could see that in disposition he was as far as possible from being either. Indeed, his disposition was evidently very like that of her own grandfather (who wasn't great at all, at least not in comparison with this one), even to the bag of marshmallows in his pocket. Sara could see it sticking out - but such enormous marshmallows! Why, each one was larger than the biggest, fattest sofa-pillow Sara had ever seen. And, of course, beside the marshmallows, the Great-Great-Great-Great had beautiful white hair, and twinkling eyes, and all the usual equipment of a grandfather.

"Why, good afternoon, Pirlaps," said the Great-Great-Great-Great, in a little high, cracked voice that seemed very odd. ("As they get greater, their voices get smaller," explained Pirlaps, who had noticed that Sara jumped when the old gentleman spoke.) "Would you like a marshmallow?" he continued, tossing one down to her; and Sara saw that it would have tipped her over, as Jimmie's missiles sometimes did when they had a pillow-fight, if Pirlaps had not caught it. While she was wondering what would be the polite way to eat so huge a marshmallow, she saw the other Grandfathers coming toward her. She knew them because there were four of them, marching in single file, with their hands on each other's shoulders. The Great-Great-Great, who was next in size to the one on the Post of Honor, was leading, and they were arranged in order down to the plain Grandfather, who was not much above the usual height.

At the same moment she saw the Grandmothers coming from the opposite direction, in the same manner. Only, the mate to the Great-Great-Great-Great was leading, and they were coming straight toward the vacant Post. Sara watched them with extreme interest. They, too, were of quite the usual grandmotherly pattern, but were equally variable and extraordinary in size. When they reached the Post they made a sort of living stepladder, like the acrobats in the circus; that is, the plain Grandmother stooped over, like a boy playing leapfrog, and the Great mounted on her back; then the Great-Great mounted on her back, and so on, until finally the Great-Great-Great-Great got upon the very top and so stepped upon the Post. She took her seat in an arm-chair like the one on the other Post, and Sara noticed that her kerchief was exactly the size of one of Mother's hemstitched sheets. She was indeed a handsome, venerable and distinguished-looking old lady, if you stood far enough away to see her all at once.

"Well, Sara, should you like to see the cousins?" asked Pirlaps, when this interesting manoeuvre had been completed and the other Grandmothers began to disperse. "We'll be just about in time for the drill."

"Yes, indeed," cried Sara, who was very fond of watching drills. So Pirlaps led her to a level place which he told her was the cousins' drill-ground. It was hard and smooth, and marked off with lines like a tennis-court, only much more intricately. And there were numbers of cousins standing about, each one looking very erect and alert, with his hand on the back of a chair. Just as Sara came up, the captain of the cousins stepped out in front and called, "Attention!"

The cousins looked so attentive it was almost painful.

Then he called out, "First Cousin once removed!" and the First Cousin marched out very stiffly and set his chair down accurately on the first mark, after which he sat down in it with military precision. Then the captain called, "Second Cousin once removed!" and the Second Cousin marched out and sat down in the right place quite as impressively.

Well, you can imagine how it went on, as far as Tenth Cousin eighth removed; and after they had gone through it straight the captain began skipping them around. It was very lively and exciting; but when Pirlaps heard Sara give a little sigh, and asked her, with a twinkle, how she liked it, she was obliged to answer, "I like it, but - it makes my head turn around. It's so much like arithmetic."

"That's what Avrillia says," answered Pirlaps, smiling. "Well, let's walk around a bit. And then I'll show you the Strained Relations."

Sara thought that sounded very interesting; and, besides, she was glad to walk after standing still so long. So they strolled about, enjoying the pleasant afternoon, and the oddity of the people and their ways. There were any number of step-relatives, mothers, fathers, brothers and sisters, sitting around on their various steps, or carrying them jauntily under their arms. She noticed that none of them had a servant to carry them, however, from which she concluded that they were not so well-to-do as Pirlaps. But then, none of the steps were of chocolate. They were of various materials, however, even yellow.

Once, in crossing the uncommon, they met one of Pirlaps' half-sisters. She was divided lengthwise, and so had only a profile; but, as her profile was very pretty, the effect was not at all unpleasant. While they were talking to her, one of his half-brothers came up, but he was divided crosswise, and so had no back. However, from the front, of course, you hardly noticed it.

"Well," said Pirlaps, at last, glancing at the small clinical thermometer he carried, "we'll just have time to take a look at the Strained Relations, and then I must get back and help Avrillia vanish the children."

He led Sara to a distant corner of the uncommon that was fenced off from the rest by a high wire netting. It looked rather like the high nets about a tennis-court, except that it was made of silver wire, with a mesh as fine as a milk-strainer. Inside the wire, in a sort of little private park, she could see a number of very haughty-looking persons moving about.

"Don't speak to them," said Pirlaps, as they drew near. "They're entirely too snobbish to be spoken to."

Sara approached in awe, and they stood gazing at the pale, supercilious-looking creatures, who returned their gaze through monocles, lorgnettes, and other contemptuous media.

"You see," explained Pirlaps, "nobody speaks to them. Every time they go in or out, they pass through the strainer, and that strains out all of their red corpuscles and leaves only the blue. That's why they are so superior and exclusive. Of course, too, it makes them very thin, and gives them that sheer, transparent look." And, indeed, Sara noticed that she could see quite through one of the thinnest ones, who wore a very high-necked dress buttoned in the back.

Pirlaps was now growing anxious to be at home, so after saying good-by to the important personages on the Posts of Honor, they started back.

As they drew near, they saw Avrillia in the rose-garden near the balcony, looking very lovely as she moved among the flowers.

"Ah," said Pirlaps, "she's already vanished them. She's gathering rose-leaves for tomorrow's poems."

As he spoke, Avrillia, looking up, waved a blue rose to them, and disappeared within the house. In a moment she reappeared, wearing the sweetest smile Sara had ever seen.

Pirlaps looked greatly pleased and touched. And no wonder; for Avrillia was coming out to meet him, bringing him his step with her own hands.

CHAPTER IV

THE INVADERS

When Sara dropped the curtains behind her the next morning she paused in horror, with her hand poised above the dimple-holder. What had happened to her lovely Garden in the night?

It looked exactly as her own little garden was accustomed to look three days after a hard freeze. Blighted - that was the word: it was blighted. The leaves hung limp and brown from the trees; the blue plush grass, and even the blue bark of the Gugollaph-tree, had turned a most sickly green. The water was frozen in the pool; and, imprisoned below it, she could see the Echo of the Plynck, perfectly stiff, and looking as if she were in some sort of awful trance. The Plynck, on the other hand, drooped on her accustomed branch like the leaves on the trees, as if she hardly had strength to hold her loosened plumes together. The Snimmy's wife sat on her own toadstool, rigid and angry-looking, with her tail wound tightly around the base, and with the half-hemmed doorknob forgotten in her lap; the Snimmy lay watchfully at the door of the prose-bush, with his long, debilitating nose on his paws, shivering terribly; and the Snoodle looked as if somebody had put salt on his mother. And the poor, timid Teacup looked like a gentle, fat little old lady who has just been shot out of a volcano.

Avrillia and Pirlaps were standing together in the little arch, looking with passionate and indignant eyes upon the general distress and havoc, and especially upon the insolent creatures who had caused it. For Sara saw, after a few minutes of bewilderment, that the beautiful place with its gentle inhabitants had been overrun in the night by a horde of Fractions.

For there they sat, grouped insolently around the fountain, drinking tears out of mugs of enormous sighs, and hammering with their fists upon the peculiarly disagreeable-looking tables at which they sat. These tables were of various sizes, but they were all very ponderous and slippery-looking; and observing them closely, Sara saw that her instinctive aversion was well founded - for they were multiplication tables. The Two-Times table was nearest to her, being placed just to the left of the dimple-holder; and they increased regularly in size up to the Twelve-Times table, at which the officers were sitting. The whole crowd of invaders were disgustingly haughty and self-important - worse even than the Strained Relations, Sara thought; but the officers were the worst of all. From the Least Common Multiple up to the Greatest Common Divisor, from the thin, poker-like Quotient with the fierce white moustache to the enormous, puffy Multiplicand, Sara thought they were the most pompous lot she had ever seen. However, since they were officers and units, she could imagine that they might have some excuse; but what possible excuse could there be for conceit in the Fractions, every one of whom had something missing about him? Some of them, of course, lacked only an ear or a little finger; but numbers of them had only one leg or one arm, and many of them were much worse off! Why, at the farthest side of the Three-Times table Sara saw a Fraction who consisted entirely of one eye!

There was one table, to be sure, the Eleven-Times, the noisiest of all, that was occupied entirely by Improper Fractions; but aside from their table-manners and general behavior, which were shocking, Sara thought they looked even worse than the proper ones. For one of them had two faces, another three feet, and a third one had as many arms as an octopus. Sara positively refused to look at them.

While Sara stood gazing in horror and dismay, and feeling so grieved for her friends that she could not bring herself to ask anybody what had happened or what could be done, she saw Schlorge coming at a run down the path from the Dimplesmithy. He looked as wild and distracted as any of them, but Sara felt a great relief when she saw him, because she knew he was so clever and practical. She felt, too, that she could ask him what the trouble was and he could bear it - better than the Teacup, for instance, who, she feared, would go all to pieces, or the Echo of the Plynck, who was clearly all in. So she ran up to him and touched his elbow and asked, almost crying, "What is it, Schlorge? How did it happen?"

Schlorge, even in his excitement, was comforted by her sympathy, and evidently very glad to see another ally. "Why - a -" he began, and then, remembering, he cried excitedly, "Where's the stump - where's the stump? I have to tell Sara about it!"

But alas, the invaders had razed the stump to the ground, apparently out of wanton malice, for they had made no use of it. All over and around it were strewn plus-signs, minus-signs, and other weapons; and Sara noticed that the dots from the divided-by signs were rolling about everywhere on the withered grass. Manifestly, Schlorge could not get upon the fallen stump, through such a thicket of debris, and he dared not move them nor step on them; besides, it is doubtful if he could have told Sara about it unless the stump were right side up.

At this juncture, however, Pirlaps stepped boldly forward and once more offered Schlorge his step. Schlorge sprang upon it without noticing the chocolate, but he was so agitated that he put his left hand into his bosom and his right behind his back, instead of the other way around. However, it was in a loud, firm voice, with fierce, defiant looks at the invaders, that he informed Sara:

"The Fractions came down like a wolf on the fold:
Their ears are acute but their noses are cold.

They know nothing of poetry, music or art -
So why in Sam Hill should they think they're so smart?"

"Why in Zeelup?" corrected the Teacup, from above, in a tremulous, weeping voice; but even had it been louder it would have been drowned in the clamor that rose from the tables.

"Silence, impudent clown!" roared the fat, fierce-looking Multiplicand. "Ignoramus! nothing of music! Why, you don't know Common Time!"

Sara quaked; only yesterday she had got all tangled up trying to tell the difference between three-four time and two-four time; and she knew Schlorge was wrong and the dreadful creature was right. But Schlorge was beside himself with fury and beyond the reach of fear or reason.

"Oh, go on!" he shouted fiercely. "You don't know nothing about the insides of music - that's only the outsides! Besides, what time does a bird sing by? That's music, ain't it?"

But before the Multiplicand could answer, his henchman, the Multiplier, called out, "And what do you know of art, Oaf? Don't you know that modern art is colored geometry?"

"And poetry?" squeaked the Quotient, fiercely, "Don't poets have to count their feet to write poems?"

But at that juncture they were all electrified to see Avrillia stepping forward, looking so beautiful and so queenly and so transfigured by righteous indignation that even the invaders merely blinked. "Not modern poets," she said, with an icy authority that sent a hostile shiver up and down the multiplication tables. "They do not count anything - not even the cost."

It was not so much what Avrillia said, as the way she said it, and the way she looked, that cowed even the all-powerful invaders for a moment. Pirlaps, at her side, said, "Good for you, Avrillia!" under his breath; and Schlorge glared at the Fractions with triumphant scorn and continued,

"Like leaves of the forest when summer is green
Our beautiful Garden at sunset was seen;
Like leaves of the forest when autumn is flown,
You see it this morning all withered and strown."

As he finished this stanza Schlorge seemed to rise to twice his full height (indeed, he seemed to Sara for a moment almost half as tall as her waist) in his eloquent fury, as he continued:

"But we will lambast you, you straight-waisted pigs,
As sure as black's yellow and thistles is figs!
Yea, surer than squashes our vengeance we'll wreak;
If it isn't today, why, we'll do it next week!"

Sara had a distressed feeling that this was rather a weak ending, but nobody else seemed to notice it; indeed, several of the Fractions were so incensed at the bold threat that two or three of them called out, "Shoot him at sunrise!" The Greatest Common Divisor, however, merely gave him a savage and contemptuous glance over his tear-mug, as much as to say that he would annihilate him when it was quite convenient.

In a few moments they were again entirely absorbed in their drinking and carousing, and then Pirlaps cautiously touched Schlorge on the arm. "Let's have a council of war," he said, in a very low voice, drawing him a little to one side. "I have an idea. Where shall we go?"

"Better come down to the Smithy," said Schlorge. "They haven't discovered it yet."

Very quietly then, while the Fractions were busy drinking, Schlorge and Pirlaps and Avrillia and Sara and the Snimmy and the Snimmy's wife slipped out of the Garden and down the path to the Dimplesmithy. They didn't think it necessary to tell the Plynck, who was too much crushed to be of use, or the Teacup, for whom they dreaded the slightest shock. The Echo of the Plynck might have been useful, only she was still frozen into the pool.

The farther they got from the Garden the less blighted and the more natural everything looked; and by the time they reached the road, they would not have suspected, from the look of the country, that destruction was lurking so near.

When they reached the Dimplesmithy, they sent the Snimmy to sniff out the neighborhood carefully with his debilitating nose, to see if there were any spies about; and when he returned, Pirlaps carefully unfolded his plan.

"I am convinced," he said earnestly, "from what I have observed this morning, that Poetry will be absolutely fatal to these hateful intruders who have descended upon us. The only question in my mind is, How shall we apply it? After thinking about it most carefully, I have worked out a tentative plan. Avrillia, I am sure, can furnish us plenty of ammunition." (Sara, glancing admiringly at Avrillia, saw the thrilling look of high resolve that shone in her face.) "And Schlorge will have to make us two or three more pairs of bellows. Are you strong enough to wield a pair, Sara?" he asked. Even in the stress of this dire moment he spoke so kindly that she loved him more than ever; and she told him proudly that she was sure she could. Schlorge had already dragged down from a shelf three extra pairs of bellows - one brand-new one and two old ones; and he was busy at his forge mending and putting them in order. All the while, however, he was listening anxiously to Pirlaps.

"The only part I haven't been able to work out," said Pirlaps, with a worried look, "is this: How can we reduce the Poetry to a powdered form fast enough to be effective?"

This was a problem indeed; and everybody thought deeply and desperately. Avrillia, Sara could see, was already so absorbed in making the poems that she didn't even hear; but it was an agonizing moment for the rest of them. It did not last long, however; for the Snimmy's wife stepped forward and said triumphantly, in her deep, cross voice, "My coffee-mill!"

"Ah, these practical people!" cried Pirlaps, rubbing his hands delightedly. "Now for our organization. Avrillia, have you plenty of rose-leaves?"

"An extra supply," answered Avrillia, raptly. "Yassuh filled the leaf-closet only yesterday. How fortunate!"

"Then the problem of transportation," said Pirlaps, greatly pleased. "There must be no break -"

"The Gunki will bring 'em," said Schlorge, decisively. "Here, you!" he shouted; and a swarm of Gunki came tumbling out from under the adjacent bushes. "Bring your coal-scuttles!" he shouted; and each Gunkus scuttled back, reappearing in a moment with the desired receptacle.

"Good!" said Pirlaps. "Stand at attention until I give you further orders." And each Gunkus stood perfectly still and straight, holding his coal-scuttle by the handle between his teeth, and dropping his eyes into it. They hit the bottom of the scuttle with a ringing, martial sound.

"Now," said Pirlaps, "how many hands for the bellows? Avrillia will be busy writing poems; Mrs. Snimmy will be busy grinding them. That leaves Schlorge, Sara, Mr. Snimmy and myself. Four pairs of bellows - how fortunate!" He then explained to the Gunki that they were to march straight to Avrillia's balcony and form an unbroken line from there to the Snimmy's wife's coffee-mill, on the front porch of the prose-bush; and that they were to pass the scuttles full of loaded rose-leaves in a steady stream, as fast as they could. The last Gunkus was to empty the scuttles into the coffee-mill.

In a very short time they had this plan in execution. When they slipped back into the Garden they found that the

Fractions had been drinking so heavily that many of them were snoring loudly under the multiplication tables; and the rest were carousing so uproariously that they took no notice whatever of the preparations for their overthrow. The Snimmy's wife took her station grimly at the coffee-mill; Pirlaps, Schlorge, Sara and the Snimmy grouped themselves about her, and in a very few minutes the first scuttleful of poems arrived. The first Gunkus emptied them into the mill; Mrs. Snimmy began to grind violently; the gunners, with hands trembling with excitement, loaded their bellows. Even in this terrible moment Sara could not help noticing what a lovely stuff the powder was - a blue and silver dust, with a delicate fragrance like sachet powder. Surely it could not harm anybody! She felt a sinking of the heart; but she kept her eyes on Pirlaps, and his splendid, confident bearing helped to reassure her. And when he said, "A - B - C!" they all fired simultaneously. And oh, glorious success! It was clear that the poem-dust was absolutely deadly to the enemy. At the first shot the Least Common Multiple and a number of privates fell out of their chairs, as dead as if they had been caught between the covers of an arithmetic! Moreover, the poem-dust that filled the air seemed to tend to stupefy the others; so that, though there was a terrible uproar and a desperate scramble for weapons, victory for the defenders was certain from the start. There was only one defect in the organization; one thing had escaped Pirlaps' wonderful foresight. There was no efficient way to get the powder from the coffee-mill to the bellows; and in the loading much time was wasted and much ammunition spilled. While Pirlaps was looking about him with great anxiety, trying to think of some way to remedy the trouble, the little Teacup came fluttering tremulously down from above. "Let me do it!" she cried; and while they all looked on in admiration (though with only one eye apiece, since the other was busy aiming at the enemy) she proceeded to load one pair of bellows after another, with the utmost nicety and plenty of poetry-powder. A little was spilled, to be sure, because she trembled so terribly; still, it was an enormous improvement, and they all praised and congratulated the Teacup.

"Ah, these sheltered women!" said Pirlaps. "How an emergency does bring them out!"

The battle must have raged for nearly an hour; but at the end of that time there was not so much as a One-Twenty-Second left alive. The Greatest Common Divisor, as befitted his rank, was the last to succumb; and when he went down the defenders of the Garden threw down their weapons and began tossing their shoes into the air and shaking each others' hands and talking all at once. The Gunki passed the word down the line to Avrillia, who presently came floating in, with her wild eyes shining and her pale-gold hair rumpled, and her golden swan's-quill still in her hand; and everybody fell upon her with congratulations. But, indeed, everybody was congratulating everybody else, and calling him or her the hero or heroine of the day. Schlorge was doubly cordial to Avrillia because he felt that he had underestimated her; and for the same reason Pirlaps was particularly delighted with the Teacup and the Snimmy's wife - whom, to tell the truth, he had always considered very ordinary women. The Teacup fluttered and laughed nervously, murmuring, whenever anybody praised her, "If my handle hadn't been so consanguineous -" But the Snimmy's wife merely smiled grimly, as much as to say that she had always thought they would all come to their senses sooner or later.

Presently the Snimmy, who had been sniffing about the fallen invaders, suggested, "What's to be done with the remains, begging everybody's pardon?"

"Don't make such long speeches, Snimmy," said his wife, "and don't beg anything. Didn't you blow as hard as any of 'em?"

But Schlorge was already deeply interested in the problem. He began walking around among them, now and then turning one over with his foot. Of course there had never been an ounce of flesh and blood among them; they were as dry as bones - which, indeed, they much resembled.

"I could make them into first-class rules," he said, picking up the waist-line of an Improper Fraction and snapping it easily across his knee. "They'd keep the Plynck supplied a whole winter."

The Plynck! In the excitement of victory they had all momentarily forgotten the Plynck, though, when the fight was hottest, it had been the sight of her tragic drooping plumes among the blighted leaves that had nerved them to redoubled effort. Now Avrillia stepped softly under the tree and called gently, "O Plynck, dear Plynck! They're all dead, and Schlorge is going to make them into rules for you to break!"

A shiver ran through the soft, rosy plumes of the Plynck; she opened her terrified eyes, and when she saw that the good tidings was indeed true, she began to shine and smile down upon them again like a convalescent rainbow. The Gunki had already formed a line to Schlorge's smithy, and were briskly sending scuttlefuls of the hateful fragments down the line.

"I - I'm sorry I was so useless," apologized the Plynck with deep humility, looking down upon her faithful friends. But they one and all began to protest that she had not been needed in the least. "It was for you as we done it, ma'am," Schlorge assured her, looking up into her tree with his shoe in his hand; and the poor Snimmy was so overcome by emotion that he was compelled to lie down at the foot of the Gugollaph-tree, with his debilitating nose on his little cold paws, and sniffle frankly.

"But how will they get back the lovely grass and flowers?" asked Sara of Pirlaps, softly. Her friends were saved; but her Garden still looked sadly afflicted.

"Well, perhaps it will snow," said Pirlaps, hopefully.

"Snow?" asked Sara. "Will that bring the grass and leaves back?"

"Why, certainly, Sara," said Pirlaps, looking down at her with his kind, amused smile. Pirlaps was often amused at her ignorance; but he was always so kind about it that Sara didn't mind at all.

CHAPTER V

CRUMBS AND WAFFLES

Sara beheld such an entrancing sight the next morning that her dimples nearly escaped from her control while she was putting them into the dimple-holder. The Snimmy leaped up with a wild sniff, only to sink down again, trembling, as Sara shooed the little rollicking things safely down through the opening.

For it had indeed snowed in the night; the whole glittering Garden was as white as the Snoodle. The pool was unfrozen, and in her accustomed place within it sat the Echo of the Plynck, looking wonderfully happy and refreshed; the bark of the Gugollaph-tree was again a healthy, dazzling blue, and the branches were piled with little ridges of fluffy-looking snow, which produced a delightful effect. And among them, with her happy golden feet in the snow, and her rosy plumes fluffed out, sat the Plynck, looking as softly dazzling as a snowy sunrise. An army of Gunki were busily mowing the deep snow with scintillating long-handled ice-sickles. It flew up in clouds as they mowed, and another army of Gunki was engaged in catching it in baskets and spreading it smoothly down again. One and all, they seemed deeply absorbed in this useful work.

Still a third crew of Gunki were engaged in helping Schlorge reset the stump. They had got it nearly into place by the time Sara arrived. It was a tremendous engineering feat, and had evidently required any number of ropes and pulleys and things.

Karle Wilson Baker

Sara could see that the ropes were made of taffy, but she could not imagine where they had found enough pulley-bones to supply all the pulleys. So she asked Schlorge about it, and he explained with great relish that they had used the wish-bones of the Fractions themselves.

"Oh, we've made 'em useful!" said Schlorge, triumphantly. "We've used everything about 'em except their conceit. We didn't want that, so we just raked it up into piles and burned it."

As he talked, Schlorge was busy fitting the stump exactly to the root that was left in the ground, so that it would grow back just right when the snow melted.

"I have to hurry," explained Schlorge, working away with an anxious expression, "because I have an announcement to make to you - a message from Avrillia."

"Oh, do hurry!" cried Sara, clapping her hands so recklessly that Schlorge looked up from his work to say, "Take care - I don't mend them knuckles ones, you know."

So Sara sat down very quietly on the snow near by, keeping a watchful eye out for the Gunki with the keen ice-sickles, and sitting very still so that she would not disturb Schlorge. And in a very little while, indeed, the work was finished, and Schlorge scrambled eagerly upon the stump and arranged his hands. Then he began:

> "I'm requested to say
> On this glickering day
> That Avrillia is feeding the Birds;
> And if Sara will come
> She will find her at home,
> With waffles and welcoming words."

Schlorge jumped down and began scrambling his tools together; then he went rushing wildly, as usual, down the road to the Dimplesmithy. "Go see her, Sara!" he shouted back over his shoulder encouragingly. "You'll enjoy it! Go on!"

So Sara, who really needed no urging, went smiling down the little path (it was curly again, though very white) toward the little arch in the hedge. And from there she looked out upon another exhilarating scene.

Now I did not think it necessary to say that the snow in the Garden was of powdered sugar, as it is in all well-informed stories; but beyond the hedge, as far as the eye could reach (and Sara had quite a long eye for her age - her mother was kept busy letting out hems) the snow was of powdered silver. I am sorry to say it was not good to eat at all; but it was so much more beautiful than the common garden kind that I do not believe you would have minded, any more than Sara did. It was, of course, fairy snow, while the other was just the plain imaginary kind.

But the scene before her was so strange and animated that even the snow could not hold Sara's attention for long. (It was slippery, for one thing; and, besides, the crust was thin, and Sara's attention was so excited and skippy that it was continually breaking through.)

Beyond Avrillia's house on one side, in the direction Sara had gone with Pirlaps to see his relations, was a long, delightful hill; and there all the seventy children were coasting and snowballing. Every one of them had on a cap that seemed to be made of a tiny red pepper, and their little mittened fists looked exactly like holly-berries. Their sleds were of curled rose-petals, and Sara knew without being told that it had cost their mother quite a struggle to spare so many from the supply she had collected to write poems on. Sara had watched them for several minutes before she noticed that they always coasted uphill and dragged their sleds down. And all the time the air flashed with snowballs so big that they looked like the tantalizing silver balls which sometimes occur in the nicest boxes of chocolates.

Karle Wilson Baker

It was some time before Sara could disengage her attention (it had become entangled in the rope on one of the smaller children's sleds) to examine the extraordinary scene near at hand. For, on the lawn at one side of Avrillia's house, opposite the rose-garden, where Pirlaps usually sat painting under the fog-bushes, a large table had been placed; and around it were assembled a group of the most remarkable-looking persons Sara had ever seen. If they had not been so large, Sara would have been sure that they were birds; but the largest one was a head taller than Sara herself, and the very smallest was at least as large as her youngest cousin.

Pirlaps, who was helping Yassuh put some sort of food on the table, looked up and saw Sara; and in a moment he put down the dish he had in his hand and seemed to slip away unnoticed, to come to her. Sara wondered at this, for Pirlaps was always so polite; it would have been much more like him to excuse himself with a courteous bow to his guests.

"Good morning, Sara," he said in a low tone, when he reached her side. "A glorious morning, isn't it? Avrillia thought you would enjoy seeing the Birds fed, and the children at their winter sports. Avrillia herself is very busy just now; the suet gave out and she's gone to order some more. But I daresay she'll have time to speak to you after a while. Meantime, I'll tell you who they are: it isn't polite to introduce them to anybody. Indeed, I must tell you that their ways are very peculiar, and they are very easily offended; so try to be careful. For instance, you must never speak aloud in their presence, but only behind your hand, in a whisper; and if you wish to make the best impression, do not seem to see them at all. Also, if you should care to partake of any of the food, remember not to touch it with your hands: that is the very worst of bad manners. Always take it with your beak - I mean your mouth."

Sara stood perfectly still, watching; never had she been so charmed and astonished.

"Who are they?" she asked, after a moment.

"Well, the tallest one, with the high blue beaver hat, is the Popinjay," said Pirlaps. "He's just about the cock of the walk, and he's quite self-important and touchy. The one with the very long bill, and the stiff, stumpy tail that he uses for a cane, is the Redpecker. The one in the checked suit, with the black necktie, yellow satin sleeve-linings, and white patch on his coat-tail, is the Snicker. He's full of fun and a good fellow, but rather crude - for he'll sometimes talk to you a little if he's sure the others aren't looking. Ants are his favorite food, but Avrillia didn't put up any this summer, so I had to send Yassuh down to the colony to get one of my uncles for him. Poor Uncle," said Pirlaps, looking very sad for a moment, "I hated to do it; but he was only a half-uncle and quite old, and lately he had grown so thin that he was hardly more than a three-eighths one. However, he was plenty for the Snicker," he added more cheerfully, "he's not as exacting as most of them. The little lady in brown, with the bustle, is a When; like the Snicker, she's really quite a charming little person, though of an interrogative turn of mind; and they all frown on her sociable ways. The fierce-looking old gentleman with the Roman nose is the Squawk; he has a worse disposition, even, than the Popinjay. That beautiful little lady with the deep blue velvet cloak and the vest that looks like ploughed fields in March, is the Skybird; she is lovely and gentle, and reminds me of Avrillia. But she's quite absent-minded. Besides, she's very careful of her manners; so don't expect her to speak to you. Now come on, and watch them eat."

Sara was very curious, but a little timid, the visitors looked so large and so strange; so she held tight to Pirlaps' hand as they stole carefully up to the group and stopped near the table. The Popinjay, the Squawk, the Redpecker and the Skybird went on eating as if nothing had happened, so Sara felt sure she had been sufficiently polite; but the little When, who was hopping about from one side of the table to the other, cast a bright, questioning glance at her that made her whisper, behind her hand, and under her breath, "Next August!" And then she was sure she heard the Snicker wink.

All this time Sara had been aware of an irresistible curiosity about the table. It looked somehow familiar and unpleasant; and yet it was of a beautiful primrose yellow, decorated with blue roses. At last she put up her hand and whispered to Pirlaps, "The table! Where did you get the table? It wasn't here the other day!"

Pirlaps laughed softly. "Ah, Sara," he said, "you aren't easy to hoodwink! That's the Seven-Times table. Avrillia and I had a regular battle about it. Of course we never really quarrel," he explained seriously, "but we sometimes have a lively clash of wills. After we finished off the Fractions yesterday, I was determined to save that table for a memento. Avrillia hated the idea, and positively refused to have it in the house; and then I won my point by remembering that we'd never had a table large enough for the birds to eat from when it snowed. I told her we'd keep it on the lawn. She tried to persuade me to order a plain Time-Table from your country, instead; saying that, though it would be bad enough to have our nice clean eternity cluttered up with a Time-Table, it would be better than one of these. But I finally brought her around, by promising to paint it and make it as pretty as possible. She'll forget its real nature after a while, and I shall always value it greatly for its historical interest."

Sara's mind was distracted toward the close of this explanation by the peculiar, not to say angry, behavior of the Popinjay and the Squawk, who, she was sure, had become displeased about something. One peculiarity of the Popinjay's she had not noticed until she came near the table. It was that, though he had two perfectly good feet, they seemed to have grown to a sort of perch, which was fastened crosswise to a sharp peg; and when he wished to move he had to hop from place to place, sticking this peg into the snow. He was now hopping round and round the table with loud, incoherent cries, while the little When flitted from place to place to keep out of his way, and the Snicker laughed softly in his yellow satin sleeve. Sara touched Pirlaps on the arm.

"Mercy me!" cried Pirlaps, speaking softly, but forgetting in his excitement to cover his mouth with his hand. "The table is quite empty, and Avrillia has not come with the rest of the suet! Yassuh should have brought more crumbs long ago. Let's go to the house and see what's the trouble, Sara!"

They hurried to the house, and began looking everywhere. They even opened the door of Avrillia's own bed-room, which was upholstered entirely in pink morning-glory satin, with hangings of opalescent mist; Sara thought it was quite the most ravishing place she had ever seen; at least she though so until Pirlaps distractedly led her down into the basement to Avrillia's kitchen. A smell of something delectable scorching enveloped them as they opened the door. And there beside the stove, all deliciously sticky and comfortable, lay Yassuh, fast asleep and half melted; while little wisps of smoke curled out of the crack between the oven and the door. The stove was almost as big as the tin one Jimmy had given Sara for Christmas, but much more massive and efficient-looking. On the table, looking so delicious that they made your mouth water, were the ingredients with which Yassuh had been working: a bubble-pitcher of milk-weed cream, a bowl of butterfly eggs (the daintiest things!), a silver panful of flour from the best white miller, and a large silk sack of snow-sugar from the Garden. Sara had to put her hands behind her back.

"Yassuh!" shouted Pirlaps; and Sara had never before heard him speak angrily. "The messy little rascal! I can't even kick him to wake him up - I'd never get my foot out! Where are the tongs? Here, Sara, you take the poker, and help me with him!"

So saying, Pirlaps picked the soft and sleeping Yassuh up gingerly with the tongs, and Sara put the poker crosswise under the softest part of him to keep him from pulling apart, and together they carried him to the door and dropped him outside, where he made a delicious-looking brown puddle on the silver snow.

"You stay and watch him till he hardens," called Pirlaps,

hurrying back toward the kitchen, "and don't let him go to sleep again. As soon as he's hard enough, send him straight in here to me."

Sara stood on the doorstep watching Yassuh, who was now awake and grinning, and she was very much interested to see how, as he hardened, he wriggled himself back into shape, like a chrysalis that has just shed its caterpillar skin. She was sure this was no new experience to Yassuh.

Presently she thought he was hard enough to be taken back into the kitchen; and there they found Pirlaps, sitting with flushed face upon his own fast-melting step, taking little muffin-pans full of fresh-baked crumbs out of the oven. One panful, alas, was burnt to a crisp, and some of the others were a shade too brown; but oh, they did smell and look so very delightful! Considered as muffins (and they looked so like them that Sara could not help being reminded of them) they were certainly the tiniest things imaginable; considered as crumbs (and that was what she had heard Pirlaps call them) they were considerably above the average in size. For all that, what discouragingly small crumbs for such appallingly large birds! No wonder Pirlaps was so worried, and looked so unnaturally hurried and strenuous!

"Here, Yassuh!" he called, without stopping to scold him. "You empty these into the baskets and take them right out to the table; and then you hurry right back and get another batch into the oven as quick as you can. Roll!"

Yassuh, apparently quite refreshed by his nap, went tumbling out with the fragrant baskets, and Sara hurried after Pirlaps in his anxious search for Avrillia. At last they thought of the balcony; and as they ran up the stairs, there, indeed, they saw Avrillia, with her white arm outstretched above the balustrade, watching a curled rose-leaf as it floated down, down, down.

"Avrillia!" called Pirlaps. "Where is the suet?"

Avrillia was leaning far out over the balcony, gazing down into Nothing. She straightened up and turned around, looking at them with eyes that hardly saw them.

"It didn't stick," she murmured.

"Avrillia! the suet!" cried Pirlaps, laying his hand on her arm and shaking it ever so little. "The suet!"

He was not cross - he couldn't be cross with Avrillia - but Sara thought he was for once almost half impatient. Avrillia's mind came back into her beautiful eyes and she cried remorsefully,

"O Pirlaps, I forgot. Is it all gone? What will they think of me?"

"Every bit," said Pirlaps, relenting at once. "And Yassuh went to sleep and burnt up a whole panful of crumbs."

"Oh, dear!" cried Avrillia, "how dreadful! The suet came quite a while ago, but while I was slicing it I thought of a poem about snow; and then I happened to think that maybe the air over the Verge might be a little warmer than it is here, and so the poem might melt a little as it fell, and, maybe, stick. But it didn't," she finished, growing abstracted again.

"Too bad," said Pirlaps, peering down into Nothing with real sympathy in his voice. Then, with a start, "But the suet, Avrillia?"

"Oh, let's go get it," cried Avrillia. "I laid it on my dressing-table when I went to get a fresh handkerchief just before I sat down to write."

So they flew to Avrillia's pink bed-room, and there was the suet, in the midst of Avrillia's lacy pin-cushions and crystal toilet-bottles. They gathered it up and hurried out to the Birds, who were now eating crumbs and looking fairly good-natured; though you could tell by the way Yassuh's knees trembled that he had found them in a dreadful state.

Well, you can hardly imagine how busy they were kept, all that afternoon - Sara and Yassuh and Pirlaps and Avrillia - supplying crumbs and suet to those thankless Birds. The lovely Skybird did, toward sundown, trill a beautiful little song of gratitude; but she addressed it to nobody in particular, and looked all the time straight into a fog-bush - because of course it would have been very bad manners, as she thought, to pay any attention to her hosts. The little When cast a bright look at Avrillia, who whispered, when no one was looking, "Next year, dear - the first snow," and the Snicker, who was the most reckless of all, nudged Sara with his elbow and said in a stage-whisper, "Certainly did have a good time," and then snickered loud and long. But the Popinjay and the Squawk and the Redpecker departed without a word of thanks for all the food they had eaten and all the trouble they had caused.

As soon as they were gone Pirlaps and Avrillia drew a long, relieved breath; then Pirlaps tossed his step to Yassuh and seized Avrillia about the waist, and whirled her up and down the silver paths in the gayest, most fantastic little dance Sara had ever seen. Presently they stopped before Sara.

"Now for the waffles, Sara," said Pirlaps; and Avrillia stooped and kissed her and said, "Come, Sara, and see what I can cook!"

Sara thought the notion of Avrillia's cooking must be an odd and pretty fancy, but she skipped back with them to their little house, holding a hand of each. Through the windows she could see the fairy lights gleaming, for it was growing late and cold. They led her again down into the little shining, warm kitchen, where the lights from the glowing stove danced upon the silver bowls, and the air was full of delicious, spicy smells.

"Lie down, Yassuh, and go to sleep," cried Avrillia; and so saying she took down her kitchen-apron from the gold-headed pin where it hung and began to flit about the cook-table -

measuring out snow-sugar and breaking butterfly eggs into her shining cups and bowls. Then she got out the silver waffle-irons (Sara wanted them for her toy stove) and buttered them, and put them on the stove to heat while she beat up the batter.

Meantime, Sara helped Pirlaps to set a dainty little round table (not at all like a multiplication table) with pink shell dishes, and put on a jar of honeysuckle honey and a pat of buttercup butter. Then Avrillia baked the waffles and they sat down to eat.

Avrillia had hardly taken the first mouthful when she cried, "I forgot the children!" and sprang up and flitted to the door.

As she opened the door Sara heard faint little cries and tinkling laughter, drifting back from the hill where the children still played and frolicked in the snow. Presently Avrillia shut the door and came back to her place at the table.

"Bless their hearts!" she said, smiling, "I think I'll just let them stay out and play all night - they're always begging me to let them. And they're having such a good time I can't bear to vanish them. They won't bother us," she added, daintily pouring honeysuckle syrup on her waffle.

The waffles were so tiny and delicious that, every time she had swallowed one, Sara almost thought she had dreamed it.

"I didn't know you could cook, Avrillia," she said, shyly and admiringly.

Avrillia looked pleased. "Oh, anybody can cook!" she said, lightly. Sara understood from her tone that not everybody could write poems on rose-leaves.

"We do this every year, Sara," said Pirlaps, "the first time it snows. It's our favorite philanthropy. It's a big undertaking, and rather too much of a strain for Avrillia, but we can't make up our minds to give it up."

"And then, when it's all over," continued Avrillia, "I make waffles (aren't they good, Sara?) and we eat down here in the kitchen, and relax, and have a lovely, cozy time. And it makes it doubly pleasant when we have some congenial person to help us celebrate - like you, Sara."

Sara's little heart swelled with love and pride. Her eyes traveled once more over the shining little table, and the friendly faces of Pirlaps and Avrillia, and the glowing little kitchen, and out through the little window, where the fog-bushes were making long blue shadows, and the fairy lights danced on the silver snow.

Never before had she stayed so late. But neither had she ever had such a lovely time.

CHAPTER VI

THE LITTLE LOST LAUGH

Sara had always intended to take her dolls with her to the Garden, but every morning before the sixth morning she forgot it. On the sixth morning, however, her arms were so full of dolls that she could not take off her dimples. She had not foreseen that difficulty.

She had not really intended to bring them all. But the Brown Teddy-Bear looked so fiercely sad that she decided at the very outset that she could not leave him. He was not really a doll, of course, but as Sara kept him dressed in a kerchief and full skirt, he had the effect of a doll - a sort of Wolf-Grandmother-of-Red-Ridinghood doll. And the Billiken looked so cheerful that Sara decided that she must surely take him along, to reward him for being so unfailingly pleasant. And the Japanese doll had to go, because he was the newest, and because he was the only one who was large enough to wear the pink tulle lady-doll's hat Sara's aunt had sent her on her birthday. His head was as bare as an egg, because the little rosette of black hair that distinguishes a Japanese doll had come unglued. This made the effect of the hat a little odd; still, he could wear it. The Kewpie was just too cunning to leave - that was all there was to that; and no right-minded mother ever left the baby. So that made it necessary to take the Baby doll with the long clothes. (That is, she should have been wearing long clothes, but Sara's dolls never wore the clothes that belonged to them; and this morning the Baby was tastefully attired in a wide red

Karle Wilson Baker

sash, with the Japanese doll's paper parasol stuck through it, like the dagger in a comic opera.)

So there was Sara, with five dolls in her arms, and the Snimmy shuddering deliciously from head to foot because he was beginning to smell dimples in his sleep.

"What in the world shall I do?" wondered Sara, half aloud.

"What in Zeelup, my dear," corrected the Teacup, leaning out from her perch with sympathetic interest.

And then, what do you think the Teacup saw? She saw the Kewpie, who was always a friendly little soul, reach up and take off Sara's dimples himself!

"I'll do it for Sara," he said, helpfully, as he dropped them safely upon the whipped cream cushion.

And then what do you think happened? Why, the daintiest little creature sprang right out from between Sara's lips and went skipping and leaping and tumbling and running over the ice-cream bricks around the pool, across the blue plush grass, and, before you could tell it, disappeared around the turn of a little dim path Sara had never followed.

Sara stood gazing after him. She had never seen anything that looked like that before. Some of Avrillia's children came nearest to looking like it: but not even they were so tinkly or so bubbly or so altogether gay-looking. And how nimble it was - disappearing like a drop of water trickling down a rock!

"What in the world?" breathed Sara again.

"- In Zeelup?" breathed the Teacup, quite as softly. But Sara hardly heard her: she was so astonished at the babel of small voices that started up about her feet. She had been so startled at the appearance and the disappearance of that strange little creature that she had not noticed that all the dolls were wriggling out of her arms and sliding down her skirts and legs like schoolboys escaping from a burning dormitory. Not that they were afraid of anything: it was only that they were so glad to be able at last to move and talk.

"There he goes!" cried the Japanese doll, pointing excitedly: and indeed they did catch one more glimpse of the fleeting sprite between the shrubs. "He was mighty jolly," said the Brown Teddy-Bear enviously, in his deep, mournful voice; and "Let's go catch him!" cried the Baby, where it sat flat on the bricks, crowing and clapping its hands.

"I'll have to get off these togs, then," said the Billiken, who was always fat and cheerful, but seldom spoke. He was driven to it this time by the fact that Sara had dressed him in the Baby's long clothes.

"But what is it?" asked Sara, still bewildered.

"Why, it's your laugh, child," said the Echo of the Plynck, who, all this time, had been watching the scene with much amusement. "Don't you know your own laugh when you see it?"

"I never saw it before," said Sara with a wondering smile. "I guess I've heard it."

"Now, isn't that odd - and interesting!" said the Echo to the Plynck. "The child says she has heard it, but never seen it. Here," she added, turning to Sara, and speaking in a louder tone, "we see a great deal of laughter - but we never hear it."

"Well, and are you going to stand there all day staring?" suddenly put in the wife of the Snimmy from the prose-bush. "Ain't you going to go after it and ketch it? What'll your Maw say if you come home without your laugh? And your Paw?"

Sara had not thought of that. But when she did think, she realized that it would be dreadful. What would Father think when he told her his funniest story and she did not laugh?

"But - but what shall I do?" she wondered, half to herself.

The dolls at her feet set up a clamor of plans, but as they were all talking at once (except the Brown Teddy-Bear, who looked even more pessimistic than usual) their suggestions were not very helpful. Sara and her other friends stood knitting their brows in perplexity. (Sara was just learning to knit, so she had her needles and a ball of yarn sticking out of her apron pocket. She was delighted to find brows so much easier to knit than yarn.)

Suddenly the Snimmy's wife spoke again. "Send for Schlorge," she said. "He'll know what to do."

No sooner were the words out of her mouth than they saw a Gunkus running down the path toward the Dimplesmithy to tell Schlorge.

"In the meantime, Sara, you'd better dress me more suitably," suggested the Billiken kindly. Sara had never heard him object before to wearing the Baby's long dress; but he was evidently looking forward to a race and did not wish to be handicapped.

So Sara sat down on the blue plush grass, and undressed the Billiken while they waited for Schlorge. She had time now to notice that the snow had melted and left everything beautifully fresh and bright, just as Pirlaps had assured her it would do. She had never seen the Garden look so lovely and spring-like. She was glad, too, to see that the stump had grown back exactly as it was; they had even removed the ropes and scaffolding.

She took the Baby's clothes off the Billiken, and left him all free and unimpeded in his own, fat, white, furry body. You see, she always called the Teddy-Bear the Brown Teddy-Bear because the Billiken was his first cousin, and had a white Teddy-Bear body; it was only their colors and their heads that were different. Oh, yes, - and their dispositions; for the Billiken was a supremely cheerful person, while the Brown Teddy-Bear was a misanthrope. Sara had always known that he had something very depressing on his mind; and she was planning, now that he had learned to talk, to ask him what it was at the first suitable opportunity.

When she had got the clothes off the Billiken, she started to put them on the Baby; but the Baby behaved as it had never done before. It had always been a good baby, adapting itself amiably to any schedule its mother saw fit to adopt. Sara saw at once that animated babies are not so easy to manage as inanimate ones; for the Baby kicked and cried and positively refused to be dressed. So Sara, who was really a very young mother, and had not yet trained herself to be firm and self-willed and contrary, put the Baby's clothes in her pocket with the yarn and knitting needles and a ginger-snap she had brought, and set the stubborn Baby down on the blue plush grass, where it rolled around quite happily again in its red sash and parasol.

And just at that moment she saw good old Schlorge hurrying down the path from the Dimplesmithy with the Gunkus at his heels.

Of course they all had to tell Schlorge about it at once, even the dolls (all except the Brown Teddy-Bear), so that Schlorge looked quite wild, and scratched his head a good deal before he was finally quite clear what had happened. Then he turned and looked thoughtfully down the path they had pointed out to him, and scratched it some more. Finally he said slowly,

"I tell you what we'll have to do," - and then, looking about him all at once very wildly, - "where's the stump - I'll have to tell Sara! Where's the -"

But this time he found it without loss of time; and scrambling upon it, he adjusted his hands and shouted loudly,

"Over hill, over dale,
Thorough bush, thorough briar,
Over park, over pale,
Thorough flood, thorough fire,
We'll have to follow everywhere,
If Sara's laughter we would snare.
I will go and lead the van,
You may follow if you can.
Sara's would be an awful plight
To go home laughterless tonight."

Then he sprang from the stump and went rushing straight down the little dim path, shouting back over his shoulder, "Come along, all of you! Sara, ask the Plynck to come, too!"

Down the path they went tumbling - the Snimmy, his wife, a crowd of Gunki, and all the dolls. Sara and the faithful little Teacup stayed behind to see if the Plynck would come, and the Snoodle was still asleep.

"Will you come with us, dear Madame Plynck?" asked Sara, softly, looking up into the tree; and "Do you think you could stand it?" fluttered the Teacup solicitously.

"It's against my rules to leave the Garden," said the Plynck, and Sara's heart sank; for she really thought the search would be a sort of picnic, and she had hoped that the lovely Plynck would go, too. It sank clear to the bottom of the pool, and the Plynck's Echo fished it up and handed it back to her, all wet and shiny, just as the Plynck finished her sentence, "So I think I'll go."

Sara clapped her hands, and to add to her pleasure she heard just then the most delicious crashing sound: the kind of sound she had imagined when she stood at the top of the basement steps at home with the glass pitcher in her hands, wishing she could hurl it down upon the cement because Mother would not let her wear her new short-sleeved dress. She saw at once that the Plynck had broken the largest rule she had, and dropped it upon the pile at the foot of the tree; and now she was moving her plumes softly for flight, so that the golden spice was falling in Sara's hair. The Teacup was looking intensely pleased and flustered, and both of them had forgotten the poor Echo, who was scrambling about the rim of the pool like a swimmer trying to draw himself out of the water by a slippery bank. When she saw Sara looking at her, however, she stopped trying, and sat down stiffly in her usual place.

"I can't go, of course," she said with dignity, "but go ahead - don't mind me."

"Oh, my dear, I'm so sorry!" said the Plynck, hovering over her softly. "I wish you could!"

"Go ahead," said the Echo, trying hard not to look sulky and virtuous; and so Sara ran down the path after the others, with the Plynck and the Teacup fluttering gracefully over her head. As she passed through the hedge she cast a backward look at the Garden, which was now so still that she thought it looked like a picture in a dream - shimmering and bright and clear, without a soul left at home but the Plynck's cerulean Echo and the sleeping Snoodle.

As soon as they passed through the hedge they found themselves in a picturesque broken country, rather difficult to traverse, but very prettily decorated with rocks, streams, and waterfalls. Little groves of cedars, the exact size and shape of Christmas-trees, grew out of the rocks; the candles were already full-grown, but Schlorge sent the Japanese doll running back to tell Sara that she must not light them, as they would not be ripe till Christmas Eve. Sara had never seen a prettier place, but she was rather worried by a maternal anxiety about the dolls. For it was certainly not a very safe place for them. Of course the Brown Teddy-Bear and the Billiken were all right, though the latter might come to grief if he should fall on his head. The Japanese doll, who had lost a hand, was unbreakable; but unbreakable only means that you may be

Karle Wilson Baker

dropped from a reasonable height upon hard-wood floors, but not from a second-story window on concrete or asphalt. That was how the Japanese doll had lost his hand (it would have been his head, but for the fact that the accident happened while he was indisposed from neuralgia, and had his head pinned up in the Baby's flannel petticoat). And these rocks certainly looked as hard as any pavement. And even as Sara worried, the worst happened: she heard a dreadful cracking sound, followed by a shrill clamor from the dolls and a hoarse cry from Schlorge, and the grim, excited voice of the Snimmy's wife. It was by no means a pleasant sound, like the cracking of breaking rules: no, it was the familiar, heart-rending sound that makes the heart of any mother of dolls turn cold. Sara went leaping and scrambling down the rocks, with the Plynck and the Teacup hovering anxiously over her. In a few moments she reached the scene of the accident, and found them all gathered around the Kewpie, who lay in the lap of the Snimmy's wife with both legs broken. Sara ran and knelt beside her.

"Now, here, don't you go and burst into tears," said Schlorge, speaking in the gruff tone an anxious doctor uses toward an excitable patient. "I'll have my hands full mending your baby here, without having to mend you. He has no internal injuries," he added, turning the Kewpie upside down and peering down the stumps of his legs (which were hollow) into a perfectly pink and smooth and healthy-looking interior, "and you might have. Besides, we'll fix it up all right."

"Can you really, Schlorge?" asked Sara. There were tears in her voice, but, by trying very hard, she did keep from bursting into them.

"Of course I can!" said Schlorge, speaking quite crossly to conceal his sympathy. "Here - you Gunki! A stretcher!"

So the Gunki came running with a stretcher made out of a large mullein-leaf, and they put the Kewpie and his legs tenderly upon it. He was a trifle pale, but still smiling, and insisted that he did not suffer at all.

"Only it's inconvenient, you know, not to be able to walk," he explained, "and I didn't want to miss the fun. Would it be too much trouble - could you take me this way? These gentlemen, now -"

"Sure!" said the four Gunki at once, in tenor, baritone, bass, and second bass. Sara, even in her distress, was charmed; for that was the first time she had heard a Gunkus speak.

"Are you sure you won't faint from loss of air?" asked Schlorge looking at the patient anxiously; and indeed the air was pouring in a steady stream out of the Kewpie's inside.

"I'll be all right - only take me along," maintained the Kewpie, valiantly.

So they all started on again across the rough, uncharted country.

Now, all this time they had not had so much as a glimpse of Sara's laugh. The Snimmy ran along ahead with his long, quivering, debilitating nose to the ground; and two or three times he raised it, and said in an excited undertone, to Schlorge, "It touched here." And then they would all look anxiously about, under every rock, and behind every stump, without finding a trace of it.

But after they had gone a long way, and were all getting tired and thirsty (not to say hungry) they came to a most inviting little grove around a spring; and here, with one accord, they all threw themselves down to rest. The Teacup, with an arch look, dropped down to the spring, filled herself with water, and fluttered up to Sara's lips, saying softly, "Allow me, my dear!" Sara drank, in delight and wonder, and found that the spring was not made of water, but of a sort of super-lemonade, the most delicious beverage she had ever tasted. After she had drunk, the Teacup took a drink to the Plynck, explaining to her with an apologetic smile, "I served her first, my dear, because she was the guest of honor - so to speak," and the Plynck assented most graciously. Then the kind-hearted and democratic little Teacup performed the same gracious office for the whole company, one after the other - even the Baby doll and the Gunki who bore the stretcher. But the Billiken did look very funny drinking out of the Teacup; and it was just at that moment that they were startled by a little gurgling sound in the tree above them (as if a Brownie had overturned a blue honey-pitcher, and the little drops were tumbling over each other upon a silver floor) and Sara's lost laugh sprang from the top of the tree to the ground, and went tinkling off again among the rocks. They all looked after it with their mouths open, as a fisherman gazes at the hook from which he has just lost the largest fish that ever was on sea or land.

"There, now! If we had only been more watchful!" exclaimed the Japanese doll. The pink tulle lady-doll hat had slipped far back on his perspiring head; he looked as if he had come a long way.

"I thought I saw something moving up in the tree - I was just going to speak about it," said the plucky little Kewpie, who, being compelled to lie on his back, had been gazing straight up into the branches.

"Well!" said Schlorge grimly. "It won't do that again."

They all saw that Schlorge had something on his mind, and began to watch him as he took his gimlet out of his pocket and began to cut a small willow wand.

"What are you going to do, Schlorge?" asked the Japanese doll, who was a good sort of a person, but a little lacking in tact.

"Never mind me," said Schlorge, "the rest of you take a nap!"

Sara saw that his professional pride, as the leader and practical man of the party, had been hurt by the escape of her laugh;

and he spoke so crossly that they all turned around and began to try to make conversation to cover their embarrassment. But they didn't succeed very well; and presently the Baby spoke the thought that was uppermost in everybody's mind.

"I'm hungry!" he said.

Alas, so were they all! It was no use trying to disguise it! So the Snimmy said, almost tearfully, "Why didn't we think to bring some lunch?"

"Humph!" retorted his wife. "You'd never think of anything - except dimples!"

So saying, she took down a large hamper which she had been carrying on her head, and removed the cloth which was tucked neatly over it. They had all noticed the hamper, but supposed it was Avrillia's wash, which the Snimmy's wife always took home on Poppyday.

Now it proved to be packed full of a rich and varied picnic luncheon, the sight and aroma of which made even the Brown Teddy-Bear look eager. The Snimmy's wife set all the viands out on the grass, and the Plynck graciously drifted down and took her place at the head of the table. There was a trifle too much sand in the sandwiches, but everything else was perfect; and they all ate as immoderately as people do at picnics.

Sara found herself seated next to the Brown Teddy-Bear. After he had eaten a pickle or two and begun to look cheerful, she asked him, tactfully, what he had had so long on his mind.

"I'll tell you, Sara," said the Brown Teddy-Bear candidly and mournfully. "I'm so ephemeral."

Sara opened her eyes, and looked at him carefully. What new affliction was this? "Do you mean you're sick?" she asked, after a while.

Karle Wilson Baker

"No, Sara," said the Teddy-Bear, smiling sadly. "You don't understand. What I mean is, I'm already old-fashioned; I've had my day. Twenty years from now, nobody will know what you mean when you speak of a Teddy-Bear."

"I will," said Sara, squeezing his paw affectionately.

"Well, perhaps you will, Sara," admitted the Teddy-Bear, "because you'll remember. But the children won't, and they're the only ones that matter."

"I'll tell mine," insisted Sara stoutly.

"Ah, yes, Sara," said the Teddy-Bear, still more sadly, "but such loyalty as yours is rare. I have but a frail hold upon posterity. The same is true of many of my colleagues - the Billiken, for instance, and the Kewp. But the Billiken is a philosopher, and doesn't care; and the Kewp is a careless child. But I feel it, Sara; I have to confess to you that I am a prey to the 'last infirmity of noble minds.'" After a moment he added, less sadly but more irritably, "That creature, now, brainless as it is, is just a doll. And dolls are immortal."

"It's a Baby doll," said Sara, wishing to offer consolation, but really not knowing what to say.

"Humph," said the Brown Teddy-Bear disgustedly. "Babies are as universal as dolls."

Sara was still trying to think of something pleasant to say to him, when she noticed that the Plynck, having finished her luncheon, had flown up to a bough of the tree just over the spring; and suddenly she heard her speak.

"Well!" she said in astonishment. "Where did you come from?"

And looking down, Sara saw the Echo of the Plynck in the water. She looked quite imperturbable again, and quite cerulean. "Oh, I have ways of doing things," she answered, preening her feathers. And the Plynck was so mystified that she did not say another word.

Really, she didn't have time, for Schlorge strolled back into their midst at that moment, carrying a butterfly net he had just finished. The stick was made of the willow wand Sara had seen him cut; and the bag was made of two thicknesses of spider's web. "Now I'll get him," said Schlorge grimly. "Pack up now, and let's start out again."

So all together they started out, climbing hills, and jumping across tumbling streams, and scrambling over rocks. It was quite hard for the stretcher-bearers, but they bore up manfully; and the Kewpie never lost his arch, heroic smile.

Suddenly Schlorge, who was ahead, came stealing back to them. "Hist!" he cried, and all the Gunki hissed venomously. "I saw it light in an am-bush just to the left of that big rock. Now, I want you all to spread out and form a large circle, with the bush in the centre; then, if I miss it, everybody must try to shoo it back toward the middle. Don't let it pass over you."

So they all stole to the places Schlorge indicated, and then waited breathlessly while he stealthily approached the am-bush. The little laugh, feeling over-confident, must have been dozing; for it did not see him until he was within a few feet. Then it flew out wildly, with a sound like that made by the wings of a mother bird who leaves her nest at the last moment. But it was caught at last. With one skilful, triumphant swoop Schlorge had it.

And then how it did titter and twitter and giggle and struggle! It fanned its wings as furiously as a Zizz; it was as wild as a moon-moth in a net, or a bird you hold in your hand. And all the time, it was about to die with amusement.

They all gathered around to see what a darling little thing it was. Even Schlorge admired it openly; and the Snimmy's wife said grudgingly, "It sure is pretty." As for the Snimmy, he buried his face in his hands. "I can't stand it!" he groaned, and the gum-drops began to squeeze through his fingers. "It makes him think of dimples," his wife explained, in a low tone, to Sara.

"'So near and yet so far,' you know," fluttered the Teacup, sympathetically.

The next thing was to decide how to get their captive home. Schlorge was quite sure it couldn't break the net; still, he thought it best to accept the Brown Teddy-Bear's suggestion that they put it, net and all, into the Snimmy's wife's basket, and tie the lid securely.

"'Specially since we have to go around by the Smithy," he added, "and patch up our brittle friend, here."

So they made the little laugh secure in the basket, and went on toward the Smithy. It kept them all amused by the happy, ridiculous little sounds it made, giggling and scuttling and fluttering about in the basket. Even the Brown Teddy-Bear smiled once or twice.

Toward sundown they reached the Smithy, and Schlorge had soon turned his anvil into an operating table, on which they laid the uncomplaining little sufferer. The Snimmy's wife said there were plenty of onions at home in the sugar-bowl, and Schlorge offered to send a Gunkus after them; but the Kewpie would not hear of it, so Schlorge mended him quite quickly and neatly without an anaesthetic at all. He declared himself able to walk, at once, but they persuaded him to let the Gunki carry him to the gate on the stretcher. And so they all escorted Sara and her dolls back to the dimple-holder in state.

The Snoodle was awake, and howling lonesomely; but he was soon frisking happily about their feet. The Plynck flew at once to her branch and looked into the pool, and there sat her Echo.

"Have a pleasant day?" the latter asked, inscrutably.

But the Plynck was so puzzled that she said nothing at all. However, when she was leaving the Garden, Sara heard her say to the Teacup, as she slipped on an iris-colored kimono and shook down her back plumes,

"I think I won't break any rules tomorrow. I think I'll just rest."

CHAPTER VII

ACCEPTING AN INVITATION

The next morning Sara took with her only the Kewpie and the Baby. The Japanese doll was perfectly willing either to go or stay; he was not at all temperamental, and anything suited him. She could tell from the Billiken's smile that he didn't mind staying in the least; and the Brown Teddy-Bear looked tired. He couldn't talk, of course, on the everyday-side of the ivory doors; but with the new insight she had acquired into his character, Sara felt sure his expression meant, "I think I'd rather just sit in the corner. At my age a little excitement goes a long way." As for the Kewpie, Sara was determined to take him, as a reward for the distinguished fortitude he had shown the day before; and the Baby, on the other hand, had behaved so badly that she felt uneasy about leaving him. If he should act that way again - for instance, when Lucy disturbed him in dusting the room - why, Lucy might spank him! So the Kewpie was rewarded for being good, and the Baby was rewarded for being bad, and Sara slipped through the ivory doors with both of them tucked under one arm.

Almost immediately a Gunkus in livery stepped up and handed her a note from Avrillia. He made a low bow, holding his shoe in his right hand over his heart.

It was written on a rose-leaf, of course, and it had a delightful faint odor, not only of roses, but of isthagaria. Sara opened it, and read,

"We're leaving on the early boat. Would you like to go with us? We'll be gone all day."

There was no answer to that but to run as fast as she could down the little curly path. This morning it was not so much curly as melodious; but Sara was in such a hurry that she hardly noticed. She forgot to dismiss the Gunkus, but left him standing in front of the dimple-holder, still bowing low, with his left shoe in his right hand over his heart.

Pirlaps was standing on the front steps, all ready to start, and beside him grinned Yassuh, carrying the step in one hand and an enormous traveling-bag (almost as large as Sara's mother's leather purse) in the other.

"Good-morning, Sara," said Pirlaps, in his unfailingly delightful way, "I'm glad you got here in time. Avrillia will be ready in a second or two."

Sara could hardly keep from skipping, she was so pleased at the prospect of a day's expedition with Pirlaps and Avrillia. She did not know where they were going, but that didn't matter: she was sure to see something interesting. She edged up to Yassuh, taking care, however, not to get close enough to brush against his chocolate outside, which might come off on her clean apron. "What's in your bag?" she coaxed, mischievously.

"Only my extra trousers, Sara," said Pirlaps, smiling; and then Sara remembered that, though he did so many useful things (when he was not asleep), she had never once heard Yassuh speak. He only grinned and rolled his white eyes as Pirlaps continued, "We're taking twelve extra pairs."

Just then Avrillia came out of the door. Avrillia could not be ungraceful or abrupt, but she was evidently in a hurry. Her motions were rather like that of a wisp of white sea-fog that is blown ahead of a rising wind.

"There was so much to do before I could get off!" she

explained a little breathlessly. "The children came unexpectedly, too, and I had to vanish them. Then, while I was dressing, I thought of a poem I had to write about hair-pins - and oh, it almost stuck! It acted as if it were going to, so I watched it longer than usual. But now I guess we're off," she ended turning to fasten the door behind her. Sara noticed that she fastened it with a hook and eye exactly like the ones on Mother's prettiest waist - only this one was more valuable, being of gold.

"Well, it's quite a long walk down to the landing," said Pirlaps, leading the way, "and we don't want to miss the boat."

So they started off in the direction Sara had never gone before, following a path that presently began to wind down among the cliffs, giving them a blue view of the sea. Sara could hardly follow the path for looking. Before long they could look back and see Avrillia's balcony, with the little box-trees on the marble balustrade, and, far below it, the gray abyss of Nothing. It was very strange and beautiful, but it gave Sara a queer, empty feeling somewhere under her little apron; and she was glad to turn her eyes back to the sea, which beckoned far below them, a dancing blueness; and to the golden cliffs, laughing in the sunlight far and near. The path was quite steep and winding and unexpected, and Yassuh scrambled about a good deal; but he managed to keep hold of the step and the bag. As for Sara, she had never seen a more fascinating place, and she supposed these great cliffs must form a part of the walls of the amphitheatre she had seen from Schlorge's stump. Presently, at one especially wild, golden place, where the path followed the edge of a chasm, Pirlaps paused a moment and said,

"You can hear a lovely reflection from here, Sara. Shall I call?"

"A reflection?" said Sara, wonderingly.

"Surely," said Pirlaps. "Listen." Then he cupped his hands about his lips and called clearly,

"Avrillia!"

"'Rillia!" came back the wild, eerie syllables, so distinctly that Sara's heart leaped.

"Oh, an echo!" she cried, clapping her hands. "How beautiful!"

"Bless the child!" said Pirlaps, smiling at Avrillia. "You hear a reflection, Sara; you see an echo."

"Like the Echo of the Plynck in the pool," supplemented Avrillia. "Don't you remember, Sara?"

Sara was sure her father had told her it was just the other way around; but she was too happy to argue. So, to change the subject, she asked Pirlaps very respectfully where they were going.

"To Zinariola, Sara - to the City. You've never been there, have you?"

Never, never had Sara been there; and she began immediately trying to build that lovely city in her mind - the frail spires, and the rich bazaars, dusky and spicy and full of brocades and silks, and the little narrow, climbing streets. But, though it was a pleasure to try, she knew she could not imagine anything so strange and charming as the real City of Zinariola would be.

All this time they had been winding steadily down to the sea. And presently they caught sight of the boat, riding at anchor near the landing place, with a little skiff drawn up on the sand. Of course you know that the boat was a scallop-shell, with sails of gossamer; but Sara had been expecting an ordinary boat, and she was perfectly delighted. Of course it was large enough to hold Sara, as well as the rest of the party; but just barely. And the sailors were no larger than Pirlaps, though of course more rugged-looking and not so smooth-shaven. And not one of them said a single word, during the entire voyage, except "Yo-ho!" They sang that out continually; but as their voices were small and musical (though hoarse) one didn't mind the monotony of it.

The sea was very smooth that morning, and not one of the party was seasick; and Sara, who had been gazing, fascinated, into the water in front of the bow was just beginning to suspect that the boat was being drawn by a very large amber-colored fish who kept just ahead of it and just under the surface (with the sails chiefly for ornament) when Avrillia called suddenly from the stern, "You can see Zinariola now, Sara!"

Ah, there was the magical city! - for that it was magical the most matter-of-fact person could see at a glance. Of course it was not just imaginary, like the one Sara had built up in her mind, for this little city was shining upon the cliffs; but for all that it was not a common city - it was a toy one, and enchanted at that. And it was even more strange and beautiful than she had dreamed. For streamers of violet fog blew up its streets from the sea, and a wild light from behind the farthest cliff struck across its green roofs and gilded weather-vanes. Just as they drew up to the quay they heard a tinkling sound of music and much laughter; and an organ-man with a monkey came spilling out of one of the little streets, followed by a crowd of clapping children. They were somewhat like Avrillia's children, only quite foreign-looking, with green and red and yellow kerchiefs. The organ-man was not so large as Yassuh, and the monkey was about the size of a small spider. As for the organ, it looked strangely like the music-box that belonged to Sara's dolls.

Sara had never before seen a city simply swarming with fairies. Any city was a wide-eyed place to Sara; so what of the wonder of a fairy city? To be sure, many of them were foreign-looking, like the ones who followed the organ-man, and in other ways, too; still, as Zinariola was a seaport, it was very cosmopolitan, and one saw all sorts of people on its streets. Many were just natural-looking people, like Pirlaps and Avrillia; but some were of chocolate, like Yassuh, and some were Chinese, with long pigtails of black buttonhole-twist; and some were Parisians, with hats exactly like the one that the Japanese doll wore so unbecomingly. (Yes, Sara knew in her heart that it was unbecoming, though she would not have admitted it, even to you.) On the gay Parisian lady-fairies, however, these hats were charming - but hardly more striking than the many-colored headdresses, made of humming-bird's feathers, that attracted so much attention when a band of wild Indians went whooping down one of the principal streets. And everywhere one saw sailors - rolling along the sidewalks and greeting each other with loud "Yo-ho's!" (Loud, that is, for their size, but always hoarsely musical.)

This visit of Sara's took place before automobiles were introduced into Zinariola, and the carriages were drawn by devil's horses. Of these Sara was frankly afraid - they reared so, and turned their heads so weirdly on their long green necks. Sara noticed one in particular, which was drawing a carriage in a wedding procession that was just leaving a church. This was a closed carriage, occupied by the bride and groom; and the devil's horse was not looking where he went at all; he had turned his head completely around, and was staring through the little window straight into the carriage! Sara was afraid to cross the street in front of horses that never looked where they stepped. It took all her courage to attempt it, and you may be sure she held fast to Pirlaps. And when Pirlaps had to leave them in order to go to a barber-shop (Avrillia had not insisted upon his bringing his shaving things today, but he went to a barber-shop every two hours) she would not cross the street, but stayed on the sidewalk. Pirlaps changed his trousers at the barber-shop, too, whenever it was necessary; but today there were so much to do and see that he did not sit on his step as much as usual, and so did not need as many.

For they had a good deal of shopping to do, besides showing Sara the sights. In the first place, Avrillia had to go to the stationery store and get a new supply of swan's-quill pens. "That's one store I always know where to find," she said. "The others change about so that I always have to ask somebody."

Then, Pirlaps needed some new trousers (two or three pairs had worn out and he only had forty-four or five left) and some shaving soap. "And besides," said Avrillia, smiling at Sara mysteriously, "we want to get some presents."

"And you'll have to make your usual visits of charity. Oh, I know you, Avrillia," said Pirlaps. "If we don't hurry we won't catch the evening boat."

So they went first to the stationery store (which, just as Avrillia had said, was in the usual place), and then to a bazaar where they disposed of their household buying. While Sara was feasting her eyes on the strange, delicious-looking fruits, the old candlesticks, and the bolts and lengths of rich-looking cloth with stories woven into it, she heard Avrillia say, "Now a set of self-buttoning buttons, please."

The jolly little old leather-colored man who kept the bazaar winked at Sara as he brought out the buttons for Avrillia's inspection. They looked very much like ordinary buttons, except that they were, of course, more intelligent-looking, and they were on a pink card instead of a white one; also, they were in a shiny lacquer box, the lid of which was watched over by gold dragons.

"They will do very nicely," said Avrillia. "Now a thimble - a really good one, please, that is thoroughly finger-broken, and has a tractable disposition and some sense. The one this little girl has now is simply abominable, and wouldn't push a needle through cobweb - not to mention the heavy textiles they are obliged to use in her country. Now, some knotless thread, please," she continued, having decided upon a thimble after much careful thought. "Oh, no - not that! I don't mean the kind that won't take a knot at the end; what I want is the kind that won't tangle and snarl, even if a child's fingers are tired. There, that's it!" and she tucked a smiling little spool into Sara's apron pocket.

"Now, Sara," she asked, "is there any other simple little thing you'd like to have? They have self-washing hands and self-learning lessons, and such things, but they're very expensive, and I know your mother wouldn't want you to accept expensive presents," and she smiled at Sara affectionately.

Sara wanted terribly to ask for a set of self-learning multiplication tables, but she knew Avrillia was right, and that her mother wouldn't like it. Besides, how could she ever get all that furniture home on the boat?

So she assured Avrillia that she was more than satisfied - as, indeed, being a dear child, she was. And then Avrillia nearly took her breath away by saying, "Well, then, we'll go up and fit the dollies - just for good measure. I know a shop where the loveliest doll clothes may be bought for a trifle."

And, would you believe it, that was the first time that Sara had remembered the Baby doll and the Kewpie! However, one could tell from the Kewpie's delighted smile that no harm had been done, so far as he was concerned; and the Baby, for a wonder, was asleep.

So Avrillia took them to the oddest little shop, the shape of a Dutch teapot, kept by a little old-lady doll who was delighted to show them everything. They bought a complete wardrobe for the Kewpie, who had never had any clothes, and was charmed by the novelty of possessing them; but the Baby nearly spoiled everything by waking up and kicking and squalling and refusing to try on a thing! "You'd better behave, you little rascal," said Pirlaps, "it will be a long while before you'll ever have another chance like this!" But the Baby only kicked the harder. However, the little shop-keeper doll was very patient, and by measuring him between kicks they managed to fit him out with a very nice layette. And then Avrillia insisted on buying all sorts of things for the dolls at home - gorgeous oriental costumes for the Japanese doll, sailor-suits for the Billiken, and a handsome fur overcoat, of a conservative style and cut, for the Brown Teddy-Bear.

"Now," said Pirlaps, "we'll have luncheon - it's getting rather late - and then I suppose Avrillia will have to call on her poor families."

He led them to a little Chinese restaurant where a dumb-waiter with a pigtail noiselessly served them with very good things to eat - though Avrillia said the prices were outrageous. As they were dipping their eyelashes daintily in the finger-bowls, Pirlaps said,

"Well, Sara, shall we go with Avrillia, or would you rather stay here?"

"Oh, let's go!" cried Sara. She would have stayed anywhere with Pirlaps, but if there was more to see, she wanted to see it.

"Have you had the measles?" asked Pirlaps.

Sara had; she could not be mistaken about it.

"And the mumps?" Again Sara nodded, swallowing hard as she thought of lemons and vinegar.

"All right, come ahead," said Pirlaps. And they started off.

"But the Baby hasn't!" suddenly remembered Sara. "The Kewpie has, but the Baby hasn't."

"Then it will never do to take him," said Pirlaps, decisively. "Here, Yassuh, you stay here and keep the Baby."

Pirlaps saw a look of doubt and reluctance in Sara's eyes as he was about to consign the Baby to Yassuh's sticky care. So he handed the Baby back to Sara and darted into a store near by where he got some clean wrapping-paper. He then rolled the Baby, in its nice white dress, up in the paper, taking care to leave its nose out, so it could breathe. Then he handed it over to Yassuh, and Sara felt quite comfortable and contented. "Keep out of the sun," he called back to Yassuh, "and mind you don't melt!"

The next thing, Avrillia said, was to stop in a drug store. They found one quite readily, and Sara watched with astonished eyes while Avrillia purchased a very large stock of drugs. Even a fairy drug store is a disagreeable place to a child with a past like Sara's, and if this one had not had a show-case full of candies for her to look at she would have been exceedingly restless. But the bonbons were charming - of all shapes and colors, and almost as large as a pinhead.

Sara was really suffering from curiosity to know what Avrillia was going to do with the medicines, but she had already asked so many questions that she thought she would try to be very polite, and wait. Waiting was made easier by the fact that the poorer quarter of the city, through which they were now walking, was very queer and interesting. It was like most such places, but Sara had not seen many, and she was fascinated by the babies tumbling about on the sidewalk, and the clothes-lines on the upstairs porches with clothes drying on them. Once a goat in an alley looked up and spoke to her - but she did not understand what he said. His mouth was full; for he was eating a tin can that looked strangely like Sara's old thimble.

Presently they stopped before a mean-looking house and Avrillia knocked. Now, you often hear that word applied to quite innocent houses that are only plain and poor; but this one really was mean-looking. And Sara noticed with wonder that there was a red flag over the door.

A disagreeable-looking woman with watery eyes and her handkerchief to her nose opened the door; and then, at the sound of Avrillia's voice, there swarmed out from the rooms on both sides of the hall a crowd of the most unattractive children! They fairly mobbed Avrillia, all talking at once and snatching at the bottles which they could see sticking out of Avrillia's basket. They had the reddest faces Sara had ever seen, and no manners at all; for without even asking permission they

Karle Wilson Baker

began to drink out of the bottles, quarreling among themselves into the bargain.

Sara drew as far away from them as she could; and while Avrillia was talking kindly to the woman and the children (who didn't listen to her), and also to an old man who sat hunched over a stove in the corner, she whispered to Pirlaps, "Who are they?"

"Why, the Measles, of course," said Pirlaps. "I told you we were coming to see them! They live with their mother, Mrs. Sneeze, and their grandfather, Old Man Cough. Avrillia thinks she can help them, but they're a shiftless lot. Haven't a particle of get-up-and-go! Always waiting for somebody to take 'em!"

Avrillia was too much interested to notice what Sara and Pirlaps were doing. "Now, children," she was saying kindly but severely, "I shall expect to find you better the next time I come. No, you can't have that bottle - that's for the Mumps."

Sara found, as they left the house, that the Mumps were an old couple who lived only a few doors down the same street. Old Mr. Mump had once made a fortune in the pickle-business; but he had had reverses, and was now very old and poor.

They found the old couple sitting in front of their rickety grate, with their jaws tied up in red flannel. The old man evidently had a vicious temper, but he was plainly glad to see Avrillia. The old lady was more mild and tearful; and both were overjoyed to get the medicine.

As they went out into the street again, Sara gave a sigh of relief; but Avrillia looked quite rapt and uplifted.

Sara was anxious to see if any mishap had overtaken Yassuh and the Baby; but when they had hurried back to the restaurant they found Yassuh still awake and the Baby still asleep. Pirlaps took off the sticky paper and handed him, as clean as ever, back to Sara, who was very glad that she had not exposed him to those dreadful diseases.

They caught the scallop-shell boat, though they had to run for it, and they were quite quiet all the way home. Avrillia sat by the rail, watching the gulls, and dreaming; and Sara strained her eyes for a long time to catch the last glimpse of the little magic, toy City of Zinariola. She was still lost in memories when the boat scraped on the beach; and then they climbed the little path among the cliffs through the sunset. As soon as they reached the house Pirlaps sat emphatically down on his step, remarking, "My, but it's good to be at home!" But Avrillia hurried off to her balcony, murmuring absent-mindedly, "I must write a poem about streets!"

As for Sara, she sped along the little curly path in the dusk toward the ivory doors. And there, in front of the dimple-holder, stood the Gunkus in livery, still bowing low, holding his left shoe in his right hand over his faithful heart.

Sara was much ashamed of having forgotten him, and she had no money with her; but she had a postage stamp in her pocket, from which the puppy had licked the mucilage. This she gave him.

It was, in all other respects, a perfectly good stamp. And the faithful Gunkus seemed much pleased.

Karle Wilson Baker

CHAPTER VIII

THE VALE OF TEARS

Such a thing had never happened before, and how it happened this time I am at a loss to understand: but when Sara entered the Garden on this particular morning her eyes were full of tears. She had to fumble blindly around for her dimples, and when she did find them they were buried quite deep in her little wet cheeks. She would have strayed right on into the Garden without removing them, except that as soon as she saw the Snimmy's wife, absorbed in some simple domestic task, and sitting on her own toadstool at the door of the prose-bush with her tail wrapped so tightly around the base, she felt that she might smile after a while, and then it might be too late to save the dimples from the Snimmy. But before they had touched the whipped cream cushion in the bottom of the holder, two Gunki rushed forward in great excitement, and seizing her by the arms, began to hurry her through the Garden, crying hoarsely,

"She's crying! She's crying! She mustn't cry here!"

Sara had never had a Gunkus touch her before; but, though they hurried her so fast that she was breathless, and the tears hung where they were on her lashes without having time to fall, they were as gentle with her as possible, and she understood that their anxiety was all on her account. She was further reassured when she saw the Teacup fluttering and hopping along - now on one side, now on the other, and now in front - and murmuring, "What in Zeelup, my dear?" with the utmost solicitude expressed on her gentle old face. Sara knew that the Teacup was timid, and seldom left the Garden; and she realized that her affection and concern for her must be very deep, to bring her fluttering along with her in this fashion, without stopping to ask the Plynck, or to think of the consequences to herself and her consanguineous handle.

By this time they had passed through the hawthorn hedge that bounded the Garden, and could see just below them a beautiful little Vale, with a rainbow arching over the entrance to it, like a gate. Inside the Vale the view was not very distinct, for streamers of light mist blew across its green moss, and its white boulders, and the little stream that wound down the middle of it. It was rather a sad-looking little place, of course, but not bitter-looking or very long; and now and then a sun-pencil struck across it, and for a moment made more rainbows like the one at the entrance.

As soon as they had passed through the hedge the Gunki stopped, breathing heavily and mopping their brows with their hatbands.

"Rest a minute, dear, and try to keep them from falling," said the Teacup, who was also breathless, but very kind. "Of course, if they should fall here it wouldn't be so bad; still, if you can keep them on your lashes till we reach the Vale -"

"What would they do," asked Sara, in awe, "if they fell in the Garden?"

The Teacup and the Gunki looked at each other with wide, horrified eyes, each waiting for the other to speak.

"Well, you see, none ever have fallen in the Garden," said the Teacup, at last, speaking in a voice that was hardly more than a whisper. "Before my Saucer was broken -"

"She's a widow, Miss," explained the Gunki, whispering to

Sara behind their hands. One whispered in baritone, one in bass.

"Before my Saucer was broken," continued the Teacup, with a grateful look at the thoughtful Gunki, "I've heard him say that a little girl came into the Garden one day with tears in her eyes, and that one would have fallen, if a Gunkus had not caught it in his shoe. Haven't you noticed the old, gray-haired Gunkus, who always wears a wooden medal on his coat-tail -"

"Our grandfather," whispered the Gunki, behind their hands. This time they whispered in second bass and tenor.

"Yes, the grandfather of these dear boys," said the susceptible old lady. "He was showing the little girl about the Garden, and so had his shoe in his hand out of respect for her; so he caught the tear in his shoe with the greatest presence of mind, and ran down here with it before any actual harm was done. What the child was crying about I can't imagine; though, for that matter, why any nice child should bring tears into the Garden -"

"Would it be worse than the Fractions?" asked Sara, hastily.

"It would," said the First Gunkus, in bass.

"It would," said the Second Gunkus, in the solemnest second bass.

"Much, much worse," said the Teacup, in her soft, anxious tremolo. "One snow remedied that, you see; but if a tear fell - but oh, dear, let's don't talk about it! My handle is so consanguineous, and I forgot to ask the Plynck - and - and -"

The poor old lady was evidently growing hysterical herself; so the faithful Gunki hastily put up their hatbands, seized Sara by the arm, and again began hurrying toward the Rainbow Gate. The Teacup, having again to put her mind on the task of keeping up with them, regained her composure - at least as much of it as she had ever had since her Saucer was broken.

Once inside the little arch, the Gunki stopped and relaxed their hold on Sara's arm. "Now you can cry, Miss," they said, with evident relief.

"But I don't want to, now," said Sara, wonderingly.

"Treatment successful," said the First Gunkus.

"That's what usually happens," explained the Teacup. "At least I've heard my Saucer say that that's what happened to the other little girl. But here, boys, you must attend to these two she's already cried."

The two Gunki stepped up with alacrity, a little ashamed of having to be reminded of their duties.

"Mad or sad?" they asked.

"Wh-what?" stammered Sara.

"Mad or sad?" repeated the Gunki, twirling their thumbs.

"They mean, my dear," explained the Teacup, "were you crying because you were angry, or for some more or less legitimate reason - because you cut your finger, for instance, or broke one of the charming children you had with you the other day? Because -"

"It was because Jimmy wouldn't play what I wanted -" began Sara, hanging her head, and thinking she might as well get it out and over with.

"Mad!" commented the Gunki in unison, with great professional interest. "Then they'll have to go to the fishes. Steady, now -"

As he said the last words the First Gunkus stepped up and deftly removed the tear from Sara's right eyelashes, while the Second Gunkus, with almost equal skill, captured the one from her left ones. They ran with them toward the little stream, and Sara was so curious to know what they meant to do with them that she followed unconsciously.

Now this was, indeed, the saddest little stream Sara had ever seen. Its source was hidden in mist, and after it passed through the rainbow arch it disappeared somewhere, as if the earth had swallowed it. But all along its banks, where Sara could see it, sat great frogs, with their green pocket handkerchiefs to their eyes; and every now and then the most dismal sounds escaped them. Sara did not need to be told that they were Sobs - anybody would have known it.

Looking closely, Sara could see in the water hundreds of little black fish, decorated with silver dots and streaks. As the Gunki approached the stream with Sara's tears, all the Sobs began to sob at once, and at the sound the little black fish all stuck their wide, greedy mouths up out of the water. The Gunki fed the tears to the two nearest, and then they all sank again, with a great splashing and flouncing.

"You see, Miss," explained the First Gunkus (who seemed to have taken a great liking to Sara, in spite of all the trouble she had caused him), "we have to feed 'em all the mad tears. The sad ones turn into these."

Sara looked where he pointed, and there, at her feet, she saw numbers of little blue-eyed flowers. They were extremely pretty, and by far the pleasantest things she had seen in this Vale; but even they had a sad little fragrance, and each eye had a dewdrop on it. Sara found that, if she looked at them long, she felt a lump coming in her throat; and at last she turned to her friends and said what she had been trying to get up courage to say from the first, "Please - I don't like this place! I want to go!"

"There, there, dear," said the Teacup, soothingly, looking as if she had been dreading the worst, and it had come.

"We has orders, Miss," said the First Gunkus, stepping up, "that we must keep you here three-quarters of an hour, and show you the whole Vale, Miss."

"Whose orders?" faltered Sara.

For a moment the Gunki looked quite wild and disorganized. Then the First Gunkus collected himself and said quite firmly,

"Just orders, Miss - without any whose."

"But I can tell you why, dear," interrupted the Teacup soothingly, as if she hoped to distract Sara's mind. "I've heard my Saucer say why. It's so children can understand what kind of a place mothers have to stay in, when they cry. So cheer up, dear, and try to enjoy the scenery. The trip through the Vale won't last long."

Sara felt a good deal like crying again - but it was like carrying coals to Newcastle to cry in a place like this! Besides, she was thinking of what the Teacup had said about mothers. Was it possible that she brought anything like this on her own dear, self-willed Mother every time she indulged in a few natural tears?

And the more she thought of it, the more strongly she decided that she just wouldn't cry. And just at that moment one of those lovely pencils of sunlight, that looked brighter in this misty green place than anywhere she had ever been, fell across her path.

"What's that?" she asked the Teacup.

"Why, dear, that comes from the Smiles. They live just over the way, you know. We'll go by and see them on our way home."

Here was good news, indeed! Sara had never felt more relieved. But at that very moment she drew back; for she had seen several disheveled, cross, black-browed children peering at her out of a sort of cave in the rock. Behind them was a very ill-natured-looking old man.

"Those are the Frowns," said the Teacup, holding Sara's hand reassuringly. "They live in that cave with their step-father, Old Man Scowl. Just come on by, as if you didn't notice them. But remember how they look. And listen to those sighs!"

So that was the doleful noise she had been hearing, up in the little pine-trees? Sara looked up, and for a minute could see them quite distinctly - little wispy, gray creatures, blowing about in the wind. They were better than the Frowns and the Sobs, she decided, - but dear me! Why should anybody be so dismal?

They had now followed the windings of the little Vale till they came to a great wall of rock that rose across it. In the rock was an opening closed by a sagging, worm-eaten door, and in front of the door hung a rusty black curtain.

"Children don't go in there, dear," said the Teacup, as Sara stood gazing at it, fascinated. But indeed she had no wish to go in; and it was with a skip of joy that she heard the First Gunkus say, "Time's up, Miss!"

At that word, back they all went scampering through the Vale, till they came to a bridge, which was made of another rainbow. On this bridge they crossed the stream, and found themselves at the entrance of a little opening between the hills that shut in the Vale. The sunshine streamed through it, and looking down it Sara could see that it opened into a meadow full of daffodils and buttercups and black-eyed Susans. There seemed to be children playing in it, and a few lambs; and down the path toward it waddled a long line of snowy geese. Altogether, it seemed to Sara she had never beheld so peaceful and ravishing a scene.

"This way out," said the First Gunkus, touching Sara's arm,

and pointing up to a signpost, marked "Exit," beside the path. Drops of water, like tears, dripped continually from this sign; but the sunshine falling upon them from beyond the valley made them look like jewels.

The Teacup had told Sara that the Smiles lived in a peaceful village just beyond the valley; so she knew that the children playing among the flowers were their children. She would have been glad to stop and join in the gay, fairy-like games the little Smiles were playing; but she could see that the Teacup was getting a little nervous, and anxious to be back in the Garden. And, since the kind little Teacup had broken into her regular habits, and braved so many dangers and discomforts just to keep her company through the dismal Vale, she felt that she ought to be very considerate. So she followed her down the path, which was now turning into a little lane, though she walked backward part of the way, with her eyes on the children and the lambs.

When she turned around she could see a lovely little old village ahead of her. It nestled at the foot of a mountain, and it had vine-covered cottages with thatched roofs, and spreading trees that made a velvety shade underneath and winked in the sunshine above. The air was full of the prettiest sounds; and Sara, listening, thought they must come from the mountain. The mountain itself looked like Fairyland; it was covered with ferns and blossoming laurel and festoons of jessamine; and the sounds that seemed forever playing and skipping about from wall to wall and rock to rock were like the echoes (or was it the reflection?) of happy bells. Sara thought she ought to know what they were, but she could not quite make out.

"Why, that's where Laughter lives, my dear," said the Teacup when she asked her. "That's where your own little Laugh was making off to, the day you caught him. Listen - there are some as little as he was."

And indeed Sara could distinguish many sorts - small, gurgly Baby-Laughs, dimpled Little-Girl Laughs, Chuckles like

Jimmy's, soft Laughs like Mother's, and - almost the pleasantest of all, - deep, delighted Father-Laughs that almost made her homesick. They seemed to be having such a very good time up there that she would have liked to listen to them forever; besides, she kept thinking she might catch sight of one. But, though she several times saw the vines swaying, or something flashing behind a laurel-bush, she was obliged to go on without really seeing any.

At the shady door of almost every cottage a pleasant Smile in a very white, old-fashioned kerchief and cap sat spinning at a queer sort of wheel; and the Teacup explained to Sara that this was where the dimples were made.

"It's the chief occupation of the women," said the Teacup. "The thread they use is something like spun-glass, and this is the only place in the world where the secret of making it is known. They weave it into this fabric that looks something like cloth, and then cut it into the different shapes with their scissors. You see now why dimples are so fragile."

The Smiles all spoke to them with pleasant looks, and gladly stopped their work to talk to Sara, as she stood admiringly beside their wheels. She saw a good many gentleman Smiles going happily about their work - drawing water, watering the flowers, or (since it was getting late) milking the little buttercup-colored cows. Here and there, too, a happy Smile, too little to go with the other children, rolled about and gurgled at its Mother's feet like a Cupid escaped from a Valentine.

All this time Sara had been struggling with a plan that had been shaping itself in her mind as she looked at basket after basket full of shimmering, shining dimples, sitting beside the spinning wheels. After trying to start several times, she finally managed to ask of one of the pleasantest Smiles,

"Do you - do you sell them?"

"Well, we don't usually sell them here," she answered doubtfully. "We ship them, you see, to the Stork. He takes our entire output. But, if you like, I could let you have a dozen for a kiss or two."

Sara clapped her hands, and drew the Teacup aside. "I'd like to take some to the Snimmy," she explained. "He wanted mine so. Do you think I might?"

"Why, bless the child!" cried the Teacup. She looked pleased and flustered and doubtful, all at once; for she wasn't used to taking so much responsibility. "That's very dear and generous of you, I'm sure. It's never been done, has it?" she asked, turing to the Gunki, who, for their part, were so surprised that they only blinked. "No, I'm sure it's never been done; but I don't see how it can do the least harm. Why, yes, my dear - I wouldn't refuse you the pleasure."

So Sara picked out a dozen of the largest dimples, and paid gladly with two kisses. Then, though she could hardly bear to leave the pretty village, with the laughter always echoing over it like bells, she grew all at once terribly impatient to take the Snimmy his dimples.

"It will be such fun to feed him," she said.

For a while Sara was too much absorbed in anticipation to notice that something was the matter with the Gunki. Then, all of a sudden, she noticed that they were looking crestfallen and chagrined.

Sara was sorry to notice this because they had been very kind to her all through this rather trying day. She began to feel sure that she had in some way hurt or offended them; and while she was wondering how she could have done it, and how she might make amends, the First Gunkus saw her looking at him.

"I'd be willing to do anything I could for you, Miss," he blurted out, turning his shoe awkwardly round and round in his hand.

"What's more, we done all we could," said the Second Gunkus, looking deeply hurt.

"Oh!" said Sara, who now understood. "Why-why! You've been so kind to me! I'd love to repay you in some way! I haven't any money with me," she went on doubtfully, - "or any postage stamps, - or any ginger-snaps - Do you - do you like kisses?"

The First Gunkus drew the back of his hand across his mouth and giggled.

The Second Gunkus dropped his shoe, and fumbled about trying to pick it up.

"Don't we, though!" said both of them, at last.

So Sara gave the faithful creatures two kisses apiece, which left them beaming.

"Do - do you like them as well as dimples?" she asked. "Because, if you'd like dimples, I'll give you some of the Snimmy's."

But the Gunki felt themselves honored beyond any Snimmy who had ever sniffed. They stuck their noses into the air and strutted along like drum-majors.

"Dimples is for folks with tails," said the First Gunkus.

It was blue dusk and starlight when they reentered the Garden. Sara, with her friends standing a little apart to enjoy the fun, slipped unseen quite close to the prose-bush, where the Snimmy lay with his long debilitating nose on his paws, looking up at the stars. Sara waited until the nose began to quiver and twitch; and then she suddenly emptied her whole handkerchief full of dimples out before him.

Sniff-gobble-gulp! Was there ever such haste and excitement? Sara jumped up and down with delight, and everybody in the Garden laughed. As for the Snimmy, he was quite overcome, and began to shed gum-drops of joy.

"For once he's had a full meal," said his wife, grimly indulgent. As for Sara, she ran off, laughing, to tell Jimmy how funny he had looked.

The Plynck waked up from her first nap and rustled her fragrant plumes.

"Was that Sara?" she asked of her Echo.

"Of course," said the Echo. "You've been asleep."

"Then it wasn't Sara this morning - the strange child with the tears?"

Her more practical Echo shrugged her wings. "Go explain to her," she said to the Teacup.

So the little Teacup, very glad to be safe at home again, fluttered up to her place beside her mistress; and they talked about Sara and her strange adventures far into the night.

CHAPTER IX

CHEERS AND BUTTER

You would have followed the Snoodle, too, if he had wagged himself at you in that delightful, insinuating fashion, rolled over and over across your foot, and then gone frisking down the path, looking back beguilingly over his shoulder.

So of course Sara did, as soon as she had properly disposed of her dimples. She went skipping along so eagerly that she did not notice that it was an entirely different path - neither pink nor curly - until she had gone through a new arch in the hedge and found herself in the meadow, with the Equine Gahoppigas, all saddled and bridled, waiting for her.

She had known from the first, just from his general expression, that the Snoodle was going to lead her to something interesting; but she was not prepared for this.

It was clear, of course, that she was expected to ride the creature; but what it was she could not at first make out. It was about the size of a large hobby-horse, and, in respect to its beautiful, wavy mane and tail, much resembled it. Otherwise, it was exactly like a grasshopper. And it was rearing and snorting in a most alarming manner. As Sara stood considering, however, she caught a backward look out of its wild eyes that said, "Oh, come on; it's all a joke."

So Sara took her seat in the saddle. Just as she gathered up the reins the Snoodle leaped up behind her - exactly as the trained dog in the circus leaps up behind the monkey on the big Newfoundland. (Only, don't fall into the error of thinking that the Snoodle was a dog; you remember his mother was a snail.)

It was a novel and exhilarating sensation to Sara (that means the way you feel when you shoot the chutes at the Park) to go bounding through the sunny air on the back of the Gahoppigas. The soft wind whistled through her hair, and blew past her so strongly that she was not even conscious of the Snoodle's drawback, though he sat so close to her. At the end of every leap the Gahoppigas rested for an instant upon a daisy head, and Sara saw that the heads of these daisies were as big as her own.

Now, though Sara was really a nice child, there were two things she had always been rather greedy about: and they were flowers and butterflies. She had often wished, of a spring morning, wandering along her own garden paths, and gazing at the velvety brightness of the daisies, and the marvelous patterns of the butterflies who uncoiled their long tongues above them, that she might some day discover a meadow full of flowers as large as moons, perpetually fluttered over by butterflies as big as peacocks! Here, at last, were just such flowers; and since the grasshoppers were as large as hobby-horses - no, it was not a grasshopper, it was an Equine Gahoppigas! Still, it was more like a grasshopper than anything else she had ever seen.

You must not be surprised that Sara's thoughts were quite jerky and disconnected, for she had never before traversed a meadow in soaring leaps, with only a minute now and then to take breath - and even that minute spent among the flying yellow hair of a swaying daisy. Still, all through the enjoyment and excitement, she managed to keep tight hold of one wish - if only there would be butterflies as big as peacocks!

Well, there were, of course; on that side of the ivory doors you

Karle Wilson Baker

cannot wish for anything as hard as Sara did without getting your wish. To be sure, they must have been there long before Sara wished; for the Butterfly Country on which Sara now rested her astonished eyes had the look of a long-settled community. I need not tell you that it was so beautiful it fairly took your breath: you would know that it had to be, with those great flowers nodding everywhere, and those great gay wings drifting, and sailing, and soaring, and zigzagging, and crossing over them. But, all of a sudden, Sara made a discovery that stopped her heart in a breath. In a country where the butterflies were as big as peacocks, the caterpillars were as big as boa-constrictors! Sara didn't know the exact size of a boa-constrictor, having met them only in her Geography: but surely they couldn't be any bigger than these! Certainly they were big enough to swallow her as easily as the big black snake Jimmy had killed swallowed the egg.

Now, if you can imagine a country inhabited by sea-serpents, of bright green and brown and pink and yellow, with all kinds of assorted horns and knobs and prickles, you can imagine what Sara saw as the Gahoppigas took its last flying leap and alighted on a flaming marigold at the foot of the palace-steps. Well, of course you would have to imagine the palace, too; and part of it would be quite hard to imagine. It was a gorgeous place, of a beautiful amber color, and was built of solid blocks of honey-comb, - which, however, had been treated by the builders so that they had a hard glaze, to prevent the wings and feet of the butterflies from sticking when they touched the walls. The roof was a woven affair, very cunningly made so that the top surface was a sort of thatch of flower-stems, while the ceiling was a solid sheet of flowers. Of course, in this climate, they were always fresh. The butterflies had their beds on the ceiling; indeed, as Sara arrived rather early, a few roistering young blades who had been out late the night before were still hanging with closed wings from the roof, fast asleep.

Sara could see all this through the open door, which was made of an enameled lily-pad (extra-size, like the other things in this luscious place). But the thing that startled her most, and that you would have found it most difficult to imagine, was the strange way in which the roof was supported.

A very elegant butterfly, who seemed to be an officer in uniform, was standing on his hind legs at the right of the entrance. His waist was very slim, his wings were very rich, and he was curling and uncurling his proboscis languidly. Sara slid off the Gahoppigas and approached as near as she dared.

At that moment a little gong sounded somewhere (like a temple-gong in a Japanese fairy-story) and the Butterfly-Officer straightened up and called out in a sharp, military voice, "Shift Three!"

Instantly the caterpillars that were supporting the roof began wriggling out from under it, and a new relay that appeared as if by magic began taking their places, planting their tails firmly on the floor and adjusting their heads against the ceiling, and pressing upward by making their long bodies very stiff and straight. Of course they did not all do it at once, or the roof would have floated off into the sky; on the other hand, they relieved each other a few at a time, with admirable precision and with no disorder whatever, as if they had had long drill in this complicated manoeuvre.

The caterpillars who had been relieved seemed to be very much relieved indeed; they stretched out their long, cramped bodies luxuriously, and went lumbering off together by twos and threes, with their hands in their pockets. Sara started to follow a bristly comma-caterpillar who went off alone, but he was so big that she just couldn't make up her mind so do it. She had once fed one for three weeks in a fruit jar, and she knew that kind couldn't hurt her - still - She felt she was just compelled to talk to somebody; but she believed she would rather try the Butterfly-Officer who was on duty at the entrance. He looked bored and supercilious, but his wings were beautiful.

She drew near after a while and said, as pleasantly as she could, "Good-morning!"

"Yes," said the officer, without looking around.

Sara was a little taken aback, but he looked so conceited, as he stood there coiling and uncoiling his watch-spring tongue, that she suddenly felt herself growing quite provoked.

"That isn't the right answer," she said.

The Butterfly-Officer turned his lazy eyes and looked her over for some time without speaking.

"You said it was a good morning, didn't you?"

"Yes."

"And I agreed, didn't I?"

"Yes," said Sara.

"Well, then," said the Butterfly-Officer, turning away and beginning to coil and uncoil his spring.

This was not a very promising beginning. Sara would never learn anything at this rate. She must be more direct.

"Whose palace is this?" she asked.

"The Monarch's."

"Might - might I go in?"

"Certainly."

What a baffling person! He agreed to anything, apparently, and yet one never learned anything. Sara wandered past him, presently, quite subdued by his elegant scorn.

She strayed on into the palace. She was speechless with admiration - even if there had been anybody to talk to. There were numbers of courtiers and ladies-in-waiting about, but nobody seemed in the least surprised to see her, and they all seemed too languid to talk. Sara heard them exchange a word occasionally, but for the most part they simply stood about, fanning themselves and coiling and uncoiling their springs. Never, however, had Sara seen such sumptuous costumes. Such court-trains, and velvet breeches, and rainbow-colored cloaks!

Presently, since nobody seemed to mind, Sara wandered straight into the throne-room; and there sat the Monarch dozing on his throne, while fourteen courtiers took turns in fanning him with their wings. At Sara's entrance, however, he awoke with a start; and Sara was terribly startled herself, because it was the first time anybody had really taken any notice of her.

"Bring her some butter!" he commanded.

At his command four of the courtiers drifted away, and presently returned carrying a silvery-white cloth, very rich and lustrous, woven of many thicknesses of milk-weed-silk. This they spread on the green-tiled floor in a corner of the throne-room, near a little fountain that trickled continually a sort of silver-colored syrup, which made a drowsy sound as it fell. Then they flew away again, and after a good while returned carrying a pat of butter in a large magnolia petal. The magnolia petal was about the size of Mother's best turkey-platter, and as white and fragrant as the magnolias at home. And the pat of butter was about as large as a veal loaf. Of course it did not look in the least like a veal loaf; it looked exactly like butter - a delectable, golden yellow, and all dewy-looking, as it used to come out of the spring-house at Grandmother's.

"Sit," said the Monarch, briefly.

Sara sat.

"Eat," said the Monarch, in the same sleepy but authoritative voice.

Now, Sara was terribly uncomfortable. To be sure, nothing had ever looked more delicious, and Sara liked butter on bread - a great deal of it, in fact. But to eat all butter, without anything to go with it! Yet she felt it would be dreadfully impolite to refuse; and she could not bear to be thought impolite by all these haughty and elegant persons. She was just about to say, humbly, "Please, might I have a little bread?" when it occurred to her that she might just taste it, at least. And oh, how glad she was that she did! For, of course, you have guessed that it was not just ordinary butter, though it looked exactly like it. It was not even the plain imaginary kind: it was enchanted butterfly butter. And if you have ever seen a monarch butterfly as big as a peacock, sitting on a throne, you know what it tasted like. The nearest I can come to explaining is to say that it tasted a little like custard and a little like ice-cream and a little like a sort of candy Sara had forgotten the name of. And it had a fragrance something like that of isthagaria.

The Monarch went to sleep as soon as he saw that Sara had begun to eat; but just before she finished he was awakened by a court official who came in to announce, with a bored expression, that two ladies of high degree, members of families very prominent in the realm, desired an audience with His Majesty.

The Monarch sighed and rubbed his eyes with his feelers.

"Show them in," he said.

The two ladies came zigzagging in, talking and arguing excitedly; they were the first really animated persons Sara had seen in all this warm, shimmering place.

"The Princess Interrogation: the Countess Leaf-Wing," announced the courtier.

Then the two ladies, who had been talking to each other, both began talking at once to the king. In spite of their aristocratic, high-bred air, their long necks and waists and slender wrists and ankles, their high heels and gorgeous clothes, they were as angry as cooks.

"She was laying eggs on my food-plant!" cried the Princess.

"I wasn't!" shrilled the Countess. "What do I want with her old nettle? Don't I know Croton capita turn when I see it? I was just resting, and she came and pushed me off -"

"She had already come and stuck her long tongue into a lily I had just occupied," continued the Princess. "And I saw the eggs after she left -"

"They were your own old flat eggs," said the Countess contemptuously. "You haven't mind enough to remember where you put them!"

"Oh, roses!" sighed the Monarch, "I suppose I'll never have any peace. Always on the verge of civil war! Yesterday it was the clover-caterpillars complaining that the zebras were eating their food -"

Sara was just thinking how shockingly unbecoming such conduct was, and how they were all behaving more like children than like the nice, unintelligent lower animals they ought to be, when another messenger came flying in in a state of actual excitement.

"Your Majesty!" he cried. "There's a strange animal attacking the caterpillars!"

Sara's heart sank. The Snoodle - she knew it must be the Snoodle! And she felt responsible for him!

She jumped up from her silver table-cloth and ran out of the palace door, with the whole court zigzagging excitedly after her. It was a noiseless chase, for the butterflies (except when they quarrel) are very quiet; but there was much excitement nevertheless. Sara ran a little way from the palace before she came to the scene of the disturbance - and such a scene as it was! Caterpillars everywhere, bristling, smooth, green, pink, eye-marked and eyeless; caterpillars standing on their tails, or crouching in every conceivable attitude of defense; and in their midst the little Snoodle, frisking and fawning and endeavoring to come to grips with the horny and horrified worms. There was one old Hickory Horn-Devil in particular, who had come out in front of the others like Goliath before the ranks of the Philistines; and the Snoodle was dancing around him in an ecstasy of anticipation. Though he was so excited, he looked so good-natured that Sara could not believe that he wished to harm even these fierce-looking brutes; indeed, there was a sort of resemblance between them, except for the expression. And, as she thought that, it flashed into Sara's mind that the Snoodle did not really want to hurt them, at all, but only to embrace them! So she ran forward and cried to the excited populace (who were spinning this way and that, wildly coiling and uncoiling their springs and crying, "What in butter shall we do?),

"He won't hurt them - he won't hurt them! He only wants to embrace them! He thinks they're his relatives - his father was a noodle!"

At this the people grew calmer, and began to gather around her head, asking cautious questions. The caterpillars did not seem to understand, and looked as frightened and agitated as ever; for Sara was unconsciously speaking the butterfly language, and the caterpillars spoke a different dialect.

"Give me a chance to prove my theory!" continued Sara, in the butterfly language. "Here, Snoodle!" she called, soothingly. "Here - Horn-Devil!" It took a great deal of courage for Sara to speak soothingly to the giant caterpillar; but you see the butterfly people were beginning to think her a very wise, brave person, and that made it rather necessary for her to be one. So she gave a little gulp which the spectators took for a sign of bravery, and drawing nearer by inches, actually laid her hand on the rearing, plunging, panic-stricken creature! He lurched and snorted terribly when her hand first touched him, but as he did nothing worse, Sara grew braver and more hopeful, and began to pat and stroke him and say soothing words. Of course he could not understand the words, but he seemed to understand the tone, for presently he stopped rearing, and at last stood quite quiet, only breathing hard and trembling a little.

"Now, Snoodle, come here!" cried Sara, nerving herself for the supreme test of her theory.

The Snoodle sprang forward at the word, and, as Sara had foretold, threw his paws about the Horn-Devil's neck. The Horn-Devil sprang into the air, making a sort of wild, whinnying sound (the only sound Sara ever heard, then or afterward, from a caterpillar); but as Sara patted him kindly and the Snoodle only wagged himself ecstatically, he grew quiet again, and allowed himself to be hugged without further protest. Then the Snoodle, having finished his embrace, released his long-lost relative and sat down on his long hinderparts, looking about at the spectators with an air that said, "There! I'm satisfied! I didn't do any harm, did I?"

And at that the populace went wild. You never saw such a change come over a nation of people in your life. They showered attentions upon Sara until she was so delighted that she scarcely knew how to deport herself. They proclaimed her a heroine; they brought a sort of sedan chair, borne, not by the common cabbage butterflies who usually carried them, but by a Chrysophanus hypophlaeas and a Lavatera assurgentiflora. And when they had put her into it they carried her at the head of a procession to the royal gardens behind the palace, where no mortal had ever entered; and there they crowned her with flowers which have no name in our language, but which the butterflies call tinnulalia. And they fed her - not with butter this time - but with honey-dew. They fanned her with their enormous wings (as big as peacocks') and hovered over her, and murmured compliments in her ears, until it was hard for her to believe that they were the same lovely but supercilious race who had received her so coolly in the morning. And when, suddenly, the temple-gong sounded, and the Equine Gahoppigas, saddled and bridled, and champing his bit, appeared at the entrance to the royal gardens, they all took out their cobweb handkerchiefs and wept bitterly.

And, indeed, Sara was loth to go; for this strange land was an enchanting place when its people were kind. But she saw that it was growing late; and, as the shadows began to lengthen, she suddenly remembered that she had followed the Snoodle away without telling anybody. She was certainly older than the Snoodle; he was so young and irresponsible. Ought she not to have told the Snimmy's wife? Perhaps he was running away!

So she gathered up the reins and saw him leap safely up behind her; then she turned to wave good-by to the Butterfly Country and its strange, changeable, elegant inhabitants. And as long as she could see anything she watched the pulsing, many-colored wings waving regretfully over the royal garden with the strange flowers.

The ride home through the cool of the evening was as delightful as the morning's ride had been; but not quite so breathless and exciting, because it seemed to Sara by this time quite natural to ride upon a Gahoppigas. But when she slid off her charger at the entrance of the Plynck's Garden her ears were assailed by an unspeakable clamor of mournful sound; it sounded a little like a Swiss yodler with a broken heart, and a little like a dog howling because the yodler was singing. And it went "Snoodle-oodle-oodle-ooo!!" And Sara knew, with a sinking heart, that it was the Snimmy's wife lifting up her voice in lamentation for her lost child.

Therefore, for the first time, she was a little afraid to go into the Garden. But she had already been so brave that day that she had rather contracted the habit; so she drew a long breath, and, saying calmly, "Come, Snoodle!" she walked straight up to the pool.

And such a clamor of rejoicing as arose at their appearance! The Plynck was so surprised that she crowed like a rooster; and then apologized to everybody (half-laughing and half-crying) for being so unladylike. The Teacup fluttered, the Snimmy sniffed; and the Snimmy's wife - that grim, undemonstrative woman - rushed out from the prose-bush and gathered her darling, and Sara, too, to her heart.

But Sara was not through being brave. She stepped up upon Schlorge's stump, and, swallowing hard, said in a clear voice,

"Perhaps it was my fault. I'm older than the Snoodle -"

"Hurrah for Sara! She's older than the Snoodle!" cried the First and Second Gunki. And at that the whole Garden went wild over her just as the butterflies had done. The Gunki carried her around on their shoulders; the Snimmy and his wife pelted her with moon-flowers; the Plynck and the Teacup kept up an agitated patter of feminine hand-clapping; and Schlorge came running down the path from the Dimplesmithy, cheering wildly.

When they finally put her down beside the dimple-holder, very rumpled and bright-eyed and flushed, Sara felt her little heart swell with pride. For twice that day she had been acclaimed a heroine - once because she had tamed a caterpillar, and once because she was older than the Snoodle.

CHAPTER X

SARA'S DAY

Something told Sara, the next morning, to take every one of her dolls. And the minute she entered the Garden she was glad that she had.

It was clear that something very unusual was afoot. She had never seen her dear Garden look so festive. It was lavishly decorated with sun-shafts and rainbows, and everywhere waved streamers of pink sunrise and violet mist. Over the fountain, in front of the tree where the Plynck sat, had been stretched a large electric sign. It read,

"In Honor of Sara. Because She is Older than the Snoodle!"

It was made of white and pink gum-drops, and they told her afterward that the Snimmy had sat up all night to weep them. The Plynck furnished the electricity by smiling every little while. This lit up the pink and white gum-drops, till they looked like the tiny globes on the Wooded Island at the Park. Of course this was in the daytime, but the Plynck's smile was so much stronger than ordinary electricity that even in daytime it shone with quite a dazzling effect.

All of her friends were there except Avrillia. Pirlaps had come and brought all seventy of the children; he said Avrillia was coming on in a moment, and kept looking down the path for her. The minute the Kewpie saw Avrillia's children, he slid out of Sara's arms and ran to them; and all that day Sara could hardly pick him out from the rest of them. The Baby, too, kicked and cried and stretched out his hands until one of the older children came and took him; and all day long they passed him, too, from one to another, and he seemed perfectly contented. The Teddy-Bear sat down in a quiet corner and shaded his eyes from the lights; the Billiken strolled about with his hands in his pockets, smiling at everything; and the Japanese doll went over and took a seat on the steps of the prose-bush, where he was soon discussing with Mrs. Snimmy the best way to stew onions.

There were so many of Avrillia's children and so many of the Gunki that the Garden had a delightfully animated appearance. Yassuh was there, carrying Pirlaps' step and the hand-bag with his shaving-things and extra trousers; but as Avrillia hadn't come yet he hadn't used his step, and his clothes were quite immaculate.

He now stepped up to Sara, who stood looking about her with surprise and wonder, and said, "Well, Sara, this is your day. You are the guest of honor, and we're all proud of you. We hope you'll have the pleasantest time you ever had."

Sara was as charmed as she was bewildered. She didn't say anything at first, because she didn't want them to know that she didn't quite understand what it was all about. But presently she couldn't stand not knowing any longer, so she whispered to Pirlaps,

"Is - is it a sort of birthday?"

"Well, - yes, I suppose you might call it that," answered Pirlaps, looking at her in the kind, indulgent way he had when she showed her odd little ideas and her inexperience. "Didn't you announce yesterday that you were older than the Snoodle?"

For a moment Sara felt as if she ought to explain that that was only the beginning of her speech, and that, if they had not interrupted her, she had meant to tell them that she was sorry that she had not taken more responsibility for the Snoodle, and reminded him to ask permission from the Snimmy's wife before he left the Garden. But, on reflection, she realized that they did not blame her in the least, so there was no need to make excuses; and they all seemed so delighted to find that she was older than the Snoodle! A birthday is too charming a thing to refuse, even if it's a special sort of birthday one doesn't exactly understand; so Sara decided to accept hers with a thankful heart. Besides, it must be confessed that she had caught glimpses of parcels here and there. The Plynck, she was sure, had one under her right wing; and there was no doubt that one was sticking out from under the coat-tails of the First Gunkus.

"We are to celebrate all day in your honor, Sara," added Pirlaps. "And this evening, when you are ready to go home, Schlorge will made you an address of welcome. But what can be keeping Avrillia?"

They all looked down the pathway, but no Avrillia was in sight. Suddenly the Echo of the Plynck spoke from the pool.

"The guest of honor always goes and fetches anybody who doesn't come," she said.

"Does she?" asked Sara, opening her eyes wide; but Pirlaps said, "To be sure! I had forgotten. Come on, Sara. Let's go bring Avrillia."

Sara was always glad to go to Avrillia's lovely house, though she couldn't help thinking as she ran that this was one manner Mother failed to remind her of, whenever she was overhauling her manners for any especial use.

All was still about the beautiful little house where Avrillia lived, and Sara looked at it lovingly, for she had a sort of feeling somewhere deep under her little apron that she would not see it again for a long while. Pirlaps, who knew Avrillia pretty well, did not look in the pink bed-room, or the kitchen, or the sitting-room; no, he went straight to the balcony. And there sat Avrillia, in a mist of her bright, wild hair, so intent upon her writing that she did not see them, or hear them speak.

"Sh - sh -" said Pirlaps, in a low tone, when he saw how absorbed she was. "We'll wait till she finishes that one. Why didn't I bring my step?"

As he didn't have it, however, he leaned against the alabaster wall, and waited patiently; though Sara, it must be confessed, was quite restless. After what seemed to her a very long time, Avrillia drew a deep breath and shook back her golden hair, and moving like a lost bird to the balustrade, leaned far out and let her new poem flutter from her hand. For another long time she did not move, straining her eyes down into the abyss. At last she straightened up with a long sigh, and, seeing them, smiled.

"Did it stick?" asked Pirlaps, eagerly.

"No," was all Avrillia said, but her voice made Sara's heart quiver, for in the sound of it she seemed to hear the temple-bells, and the fairy hand-organ she had heard in the steep street at Zinariola, and the drowsy tinkle of the fountain in the Butterfly Palace, and the little Laughs that leaped about the mountain, and the morning and evening sheep-bells, all gathered together into one sound that seemed to say that presently she would have to say good-by to Avrillia. But Avrillia, seeing her suddenly sad little face, stooped and kissed her as she had done that other morning, and patted her cheek, and said, "Oh, but I have a present for you, Sara! This is your day - we must all be very merry!" And with that she picked up something that was wrapped in several layers of silver fog and tied with a ripple, and seizing them both by the arm, went dancing with them down the path to the Garden.

Everybody applauded when they saw Pirlaps and the guest of honor returning with Avrillia; and the Teacup, unable longer to restrain her excitement, fluttered down to the rim of the pool and cried excitedly, "Now let's give the presents!"

Then something happened that came near turning the fete into a tragedy; for the Teacup lost her balance in the excitement, and splashed right over into the pool! The Plynck screamed, Schlorge whistled, the Gunki came running from every direction; but it was the Echo who saved the Teacup's life. With great presence of mind she spread out her cerulean plumes so that the Teacup settled upon them harmlessly, instead of crashing down upon the hard emerald bottom and shattering to bits. Then, of course, Schlorge could very easily reach down and draw her out.

The poor Teacup was naturally very much upset. "If my handle had not been so consanguineous - " she quavered, again and again. But, on the whole, considering her age and her timid disposition, they were all rather surprised at her fortitude.

Schlorge, who was still holding her, was looking very grave. "Sara will have to frown on her," he said, "as she did on the Zizz."

"But I can't frown, today," cried Sara, in dismay.

"I know it's hard," said Schlorge.

"Or at the Teacup!" pleaded Sara.

"It's your duty, Sara," said the Echo.

"Oh, dear, it's putting off the presents!" sighed one of the oldest of Avrillia's children; then, as she looked at the poor little gentle, bedraggled Teacup, with her consanguineous handle, she felt ashamed of herself, and hid behind her mother's drapery.

As for Sara, she was indeed in distress. "If some of you would only think of something to make me frown - I can't even think of any disagreeable things today!"

"You're frowning now!" suddenly cried the First Gunkus, waving his shoe; and they all forgave him his lack of respectfulness, because he was plainly so excited.

"Hold her up, Schlorge!" cried Pirlaps, running forward. "There - Sara - hold that expression - just a moment. Fix your eyes here - on this leaf! And keep your mind firmly on this thought: 'The Disagreeable Necessity of Frowning in the Presence of Presents.'"

Sara remembered how brave and useful she had been the day before, and concentrated her mind by a really tremendous effort. And she was soon rewarded; for in a few minutes everybody was clapping hands and waving handkerchiefs and crying, "She's dry! She's dry! Three cheers for Sara!"

Sure enough, the little Teacup was dry enough to flutter back to her perch, on which she sat throwing kisses to Sara. And then Pirlaps came forward, and taking Sara by the hand, said, "Come, Sara."

He then began leading her in a sort of triumphal march around the pool, while the rest fell in behind them and formed a procession. As there were so many of the Gunki and Avrillia's children it was quite a long procession, so that the only way they could tell the head from the tail of it was by remembering that Sara was the head and that the Snimmy's wife was the tail. The Echo, who could not leave the pool to march, spread out the lyre-shaped feathers on the top of her head and played the most beautiful rippling chords for them to march by.

And suddenly, when they had gone three times around the fountain, Pirlaps said, "Take the seat of honor, Sara, and receive our gifts." And there, in front of the Gugollaph-tree, was an enormous frosted cake, as big around as a wagon-wheel.

Karle Wilson Baker

Sara was sure it had not been there when the march began. She would have rubbed her eyes, had she not felt that such a conventional proceeding would be wholly inadequate.

"Take your seat, Sara," said Pirlaps kindly, enjoying her delight and astonishment.

Sara came to herself with a start. "Wh-where?" she asked. She was anxious not to appear awkward, but she did not see any particular place to sit.

"On the cake, dear, of course," said Pirlaps, who seemed never to tire of smiling at her odd little questions.

Sara had never done this before, but she was willing to try; and she was just about to climb upon the cake when another thought deterred her.

"But the candles? Won't my dress catch?"

"Try and see," said Pirlaps; but Avrillia whispered in her ear, "They aren't flames, dear: they're only colored perfumes."

So, reassured, Sara took her seat on the cake; and at once she saw that it made a very nice sort of throne. The frosting was resilient, but firm; and she now saw that the candles were arranged so that they made a sort of semicircle about her. Just as Avrillia had said, she could pass her hands across their wicks without being burned at all; they only winked and breathed out sweet odors - each flame a different color and scent. They were as tall as her head, as she sat among them; and the one at her right ear was of isthagaria, while the one on the left faintly suggested tinnulalia-flowers.

Before she had finished examining the candles, the Plynck flew down with the first present. "A lock of my hair," she said, looking eager, but a little embarrassed; and she actually perched on the rim of the pool while Sara unwrapped it, so that she might see whether or not she was pleased. But I do not need to tell you that Sara was; for it was one of her loveliest tail-feathers, a rich, curling plume of the deepest rose, from which sweet odors were shaken out as Sara lifted it to the light. Weeks afterward, when Sara astonished her mother by begging for the pink plume on her prettiest hat, what she was really pining for was a lock of the Plynck's hair.

Avrillia came next with her present. It was a little urn of jade and ivory, and it was full to the top of dried poems written on rose-leaves. Have you ever seen the quaint rose-jars some old-fashioned ladies have in their parlors? Well, some one of them, when she was little, saw one of Avrillia's poem-jars; and she made these others in a homesick effort to imitate it. And the fragrance - like nothing else you ever smelled - is the perfume of Avrillia's poems, as nearly as that little old-fashioned lady, after she grew up, could remember it.

You would not expect me to remember all of the presents Sara got that day. But a good many I can remember. Pirlaps brought her a picture he had painted; a very beautiful view of Nothing from Avrillia's balcony. Yassuh brought her a delicious Crumb; it was wrapped in a sticky paper covered with his finger-prints, but inside the paper was one of Avrillia's exquisite napkins of embroidered mist. The First Gunkus, remembering how she had loved the mountain, brought her a little live Laugh. He had climbed the mountain and trapped it for her, and made her a little cage to take it home with. It was very funny to hear it tittering about inside. The rest of the Gunki had clubbed together and bought her a gold-headed tuning-fork, so that she might be sure their answers were in tune. The Snimmy's wife brought her three large onions, neatly hemmed and tied in a bouquet with purple ribbon; the Snimmy himself a striped paper bag full of gum-drops. And the Snoodle's present was too cunning for anything! It was a little silver plum-extractor. With it a child could extract all the fattest raisins from her piece of mince-pie or portion of rice pudding without having to bother with the uninteresting remainder and being reprimanded; for the ingenious little instrument was invisible to adults. All the other presents were marked "For Sara, with our congratulations, because she is older than the Snoodle." But this one was marked, in a round, childish hand, "For my dear Sara - because she is older than me."

But the grand surprise came when, near the last, four Gunki hurried in bearing a large chest, which they placed at Sara's feet. "It came by the Gahoppigas Express, Miss, with no message," they explained. And when Sara opened it she found that it was full of butterfly money - the loveliest pieces of gold and silver that the frittilaries and papilios had collected from their own wings. Just inside the lid was a lily leaf bearing the inscription,

"For Sara, from a grateful Nation,
Because she is older than the Snoodle."

Sara distributed handfuls of the beautiful little coins among them and again they cheered her for her generosity. Sara felt that she really did not deserve the cheering, however, as she seemed to have as many as ever - even after she had filled Mrs. Snimmy's apron and a shoe apiece for each Gunkus.

When the excitement over the money had subsided a little, Pirlaps announced; "The Banquet is now ready!" and again offering Sara his arm, he led her at the head of another procession three times around the fountain; and the third time, as before, there beside the cake was the banquet table - all spread and loaded down and glittering. Of course it was quite a long table, with a good many covers; there had to be one for each of Avrillia's children and for every one of the Gunki. The covers were very thin (being made of cobweb, of course) still, having so many, spread one on top of the other, made the table quite high, so that there were step-ladders instead of chairs. As there was a step-ladder for each guest, and as they were made of gold and silver, arranged alternately, the effect was very unique and elaborate.

Sara, being the guest of honor, was assigned the most

inconspicuous place, three step-ladders south of the centre. When they were seated, and Sara's mouth was fairly watering at the sight of all the fairy delicacies the table displayed, Pirlaps, as master of ceremonies, rose and said, "You understand, Sara, that, on occasions like this, the guest of honor eats nothing but Toast."

Now, just imagine how disappointed Sara was! She really was having a hard time to wink back the tears, when Avrillia, who often understood more than the others, leaned over and whispered in her ear, "Wait till you taste it, Sara!"

Avrillia's eyes sparkled so that Sara was quite reassured; besides, she suddenly remembered the butterfly butter, and how her distress had been turned into rapture on that occasion. And when Avrillia added, "Besides, you have Birdsong wine with it!" she felt as happy as ever, and quite confident that there would be some delightful surprise about it.

When Pirlaps announced the first Toast, however, and the first slice walked heavily out from behind the little screen at the toastmaster's elbow, Sara again felt a sinking of the heart; for, except that he walked on his lower right-hand corner, as he had been trained to do, and made a rather awkward and laborious bow when his name was announced, he looked otherwise so exactly like a plain, brown, fat, every-day-in-the-year piece of breakfast toast that it was hard to be enthusiastic about him - at least in the presence of all the exotic-looking dainties the other guests were to have! However, Sara made a great effort, and settled herself to listen to the Toasts politely. The name of this Toast was "Sara's Day - Because She is Older than the Snoodle," and the Plynck responded to it. The way she responded was this: the Toast balanced himself with difficulty on his lower corner, and said, in a throaty voice, "How do you do, Madame Plynck?" and the Plynck bowed (much more gracefully) and responded, "How do you do, Toast?" And then she made a speech on the Toast's subject. While she was making the speech (which was lovely - she fairly soared) the Toast tottered over to Sara's plate and lay down in it, without any further sign of life or animation. Avrillia leaned over and Whispered, "Eat it, Sara," and then Sara did. And she didn't have any trouble keeping from being disappointed, after that. For, just as Avrillia had hinted, the toast, in spite of its appearance, was really Angel Food cake; and as she ate it, Sara found at her elbow a bottle marked "Birdsong Wine - Bluebird." As the Gunki were all eating, they couldn't wait on her, so she poured it into her glass herself; and when she had taken a sip, it tasted just like April! You may imagine that, from that time on, Sara had no further anxiety about what she was to eat, and that her mind was now entirely free to enjoy the Toasts. The second Toast was announced, indeed, before she had recovered from her first surprise and delight. The subject of this Toast was, "Sara's Dimples - May I Never Get Them"; and of course it was responded to by the Snimmy. There was no variety either in the looks or in the performance of the Toasts; I must admit that they were very heavy, awkward, and short of breath, and were as much alike as the trained sea-lions at a circus. However, you felt that, like the sea-lions, they were doing very well to perform at all. (Avrillia whispered to Sara that Pirlaps, as toastmaster, had spent days and days preparing them; so Sara suspected that Pirlaps, at least, had known all along that she was older than the Snoodle.) The speeches, on the other hand, were marvels of variety and interest. The Snimmy's, of course, was sad - even heartrending; and he was sniffing before he had finished saying, "How do you do, Toast?" and shedding gum-drops like hail-stones before he was half through. His Toast, however, was orange-cake, unusually delicious; and the wine served with it was a sparkling cherry-colored beverage marked "Cardinal." It was so heady that it even had a topknot, and it served admirably to counteract the depressing effect of the Snimmy's speech. The next Toast was responded to by the First and Second Gunki; and its subject was, "Sara's Tears - May There Be No Mad and Few Sad." The speech was in the form of a duet, rendered by the Gunki with deep feeling, and accompanied by the Plynck and her Echo with liquid-sounding arpeggios on their lyres, that were most appropriate. The Toast was old-fashioned jelly-cake, with Robinsong wine. Avrillia responded to a thin slice, whose subject was "Nothing"; everybody clapped when this subject was announced, for they felt that the subject was in the hands of an authority, and would be handled in a masterly manner. Nor were they disappointed; Avrillia's speech was in the form of a long poem, which she recited from memory, looking very wild and lovely. The Toast was silver-cake, with Veerie wine. Pirlaps himself, although he was toastmaster, responded to a Toast called "Sara's Questions - Bless Their Hearts!" and his Toast was chocolate-cake, with Wren wine. The Snoodle was too young to make a speech, but they had taught him to respond to a simple little Toast, "On Being Older than Snoodles," and it was very charming to hear him lisp, "How do you do, Toast?" like the others. His Toast was a plum-cake; and you should have seen how pleased he was when Sara took out the little silver plum-extractor, and used it like an adept! And the Teacup, having responded to a Toast with the subject, "If Only My Saucer Could Have Known Sara," made a very graceful but agitated little speech that brought out many cobweb pocket-handkerchiefs.

Of course that is not all the Toasts, nor even half of them; they kept it up until it was growing quite late, and at last Pirlaps said,

"Sara, Schlorge did not bring you a present or respond to a Toast, because he has made you an address of welcome. You have spent many happy days with us, and will soon be leaving. The time has come at last for us to bid you welcome. We will not dwell on the natural sadness of the occasion; rather, let us rejoice in the delights we have enjoyed together, and hope for a recurrence of these fair and memorable days. Sehlorge!"

Schlorge, overcome with pride and embarrassment, rose from his seat. He started around the pool with much dignity; then his composure suddenly gave way. "Where's the stump?" he began to shout wildly. "Where's the - where's the -"

"There, there, Schlorge, you're walking right to it," said Pirlaps, soothingly, hastening after him and laying a hand upon his arm. Then, as Schlorge scrambled upon it, Pirlaps raised his hand to command attention.

"Schlorge wishes me to state," he said, in his pleasant, clear voice, "that the gesture he will now make goes with the first line of his address. He cannot make it at that point because his hands will be already arranged. But I will request that you all observe it carefully, and hold it in mind until it is needed."

Thereupon Schlorge made a large, deliberate, comprehensive gesture. It included the pool, the Gugollaph-tree, the prose-bush - not only the whole Garden, in fact, but the lovely amphitheatre beyond it. Moreover, it seemed to Sara to include even more distant things; the Rainbow Vale and the Butterfly Country, and the colony where lived the relations of Pirlaps, and the Laughter Mountain and Avrillia's house and the magic toy City of Zinariola.

At last, having concluded his gesture, Schlorge arranged his hands and began in a loud voice:

"A little girl's mind is a place like this -
At least, that of one little dear girl is:
Full of quaint little thoughts made of sugar and spice,
And queer little notions like little white mice.

"But a little boy's mind is not nearly so neat,
And a little boy's fancies are scarcely so sweet:
So we'll give you a tale next, if fortune avails,
Full of snapses and snailses and puppy-dog's tails."

Then, for the last time, Schlorge went running wildly down the dear, familiar path toward the Dimplesmithy.

"Come again, Sara!" he shouted back, excitedly, over his shoulder. "Come again! And bring Jimmy!"

Sara knew that he could not bear to tell her good-by; and, suddenly, she felt the same way about them all. They had been so kind to her! So she began to throw kisses to them all, and then, suddenly, slipped down from her step-ladder. Her dollies jumped down and gathered about her, and with them all at her heels she went running past the dimple-holder and out through the ivory gates.

And the last thing she saw, when she turned to throw her last kiss, was the Echo, who, overcome by emotion, had at last climbed clear out upon the rim of the pool, where she sat waving her plumes to Sara in plain sight of them all.

Karle Wilson Baker

Choose from Thousands of 1stWorldLibrary Classics By

A. M. Barnard
Ada Leverson
Adolphus William Ward
Aesop
Agatha Christie
Alexander Aaronsohn
Alexander Kielland
Alexandre Dumas
Alfred Gatty
Alfred Ollivant
Alice Duer Miller
Alice Turner Curtis
Alice Dunbar
Allen Chapman
Ambrose Bierce
Amelia E. Barr
Amory H. Bradford
Andrew Lang
Andrew McFarland Davis
Andy Adams
Anna Alice Chapin
Anna Sewell
Annie Besant
Annie Hamilton Donnell
Annie Payson Call
Annie Roe Carr
Annonaymous
Anton Chekhov
Arnold Bennett
Arthur Conan Doyle
Arthur M. Winfield
Arthur Ransome
Arthur Schnitzler
Atticus
B.H. Baden-Powell
B. M. Bower
B. C. Chatterjee
Baroness Emmuska Orczy
Baroness Orczy
Basil King
Bayard Taylor
Ben Macomber
Bertha Muzzy Bower
Bjornstjerne Bjornson
Booth Tarkington
Boyd Cable
Bram Stoker
C. Collodi
C. E. Orr

C. M. Ingleby
Carolyn Wells
Catherine Parr Traill
Charles A. Eastman
Charles Amory Beach
Charles Dickens
Charles Dudley Warner
Charles Farrar Browne
Charles Ives
Charles Kingsley
Charles Klein
Charles Hanson Towne
Charles Lathrop Pack
Charles Romyn Dake
Charles Whibley
Charles Willing Beale
Charlotte M. Braeme
Charlotte M. Yonge
Charlotte Perkins Stetson
Clair W. Hayes
Clarence Day Jr.
Clarence E. Mulford
Clemence Housman
Confucius
Coningsby Dawson
Cornelis DeWitt Wilcox
Cyril Burleigh
D. H. Lawrence
Daniel Defoe
David Garnett
Dinah Craik
Don Carlos Janes
Donald Keyhoe
Dorothy Kilner
Dougan Clark
Douglas Fairbanks
E. Nesbit
E.P.Roe
E. Phillips Oppenheim
Earl Barnes
Edgar Rice Burroughs
Edith Van Dyne
Edith Wharton
Edward Everett Hale
Edward J. O'Biren
Edward S. Ellis
Edwin L. Arnold
Eleanor Atkins
Eliot Gregory

Elizabeth Gaskell
Elizabeth McCracken
Elizabeth Von Arnim
Ellem Key
Emerson Hough
Emilie F. Carlen
Emily Dickinson
Enid Bagnold
Enilor Macartney Lane
Erasmus W. Jones
Ernie Howard Pie
Ethel May Dell
Ethel Turner
Ethel Watts Mumford
Eugenie Foa
Eugene Wood
Eustace Hale Ball
Evelyn Everett-green
Everard Cotes
F. H. Cheley
F. J. Cross
F. Marion Crawford
Federick Austin Ogg
Ferdinand Ossendowski
Francis Bacon
Francis Darwin
Frances Hodgson Burnett
Frances Parkinson Keyes
Frank Gee Patchin
Frank Harris
Frank Jewett Mather
Frank L. Packard
Frank V. Webster
Frederic Stewart Isham
Frederick Trevor Hill
Frederick Winslow Taylor
Friedrich Kerst
Friedrich Nietzsche
Fyodor Dostoyevsky
G.A. Henty
G.K. Chesterton
Gabrielle E. Jackson
Garrett P. Serviss
Gaston Leroux
George A. Warren
George Ade
Geroge Bernard Shaw
George Durston
George Ebers

George Eliot	Herbert Carter	John Habberton
George Gissing	Herbert N. Casson	John Joy Bell
George MacDonald	Herman Hesse	John Kendrick Bangs
George Meredith	Hildegard G. Frey	John Milton
George Orwell	Homer	John Philip Sousa
George Sylvester Viereck	Honore De Balzac	Jonas Lauritz Idemil Lie
George Tucker	Horace B. Day	Jonathan Swift
George W. Cable	Horace Walpole	Joseph A. Altsheler
George Wharton James	Horatio Alger Jr.	Joseph Carey
Gertrude Atherton	Howard Pyle	Joseph Conrad
Gordon Casserly	Howard R. Garis	Joseph E. Badger Jr
Grace E. King	Hugh Lofting	Joseph Hergesheimer
Grace Gallatin	Hugh Walpole	Joseph Jacobs
Grace Greenwood	Humphry Ward	Jules Vernes
Grant Allen	Ian Maclaren	Julian Hawthrone
Guillermo A. Sherwell	Inez Haynes Gillmore	Julie A Lippmann
Gulielma Zollinger	Irving Bacheller	Justin Huntly McCarthy
Gustav Flaubert	Isabel Hornibrook	Kakuzo Okakura
H. A. Cody	Israel Abrahams	Kenneth Grahame
H. B. Irving	Ivan Turgenev	Kenneth McGaffey
H.C. Bailey	J.G.Austin	Kate Langley Bosher
H. G. Wells	J. Henri Fabre	Kate Langley Bosher
H. H. Munro	J. M. Barrie	Katherine Cecil Thurston
H. Irving Hancock	J. Macdonald Oxley	Katherine Stokes
H. Rider Haggard	J. S. Fletcher	L. A. Abbot
H. W. C. Davis	J. S. Knowles	L. T. Meade
Haldeman Julius	J. Storer Clouston	L. Frank Baum
Hall Caine	Jack London	Latta Griswold
Hamilton Wright Mabie	Jacob Abbott	Laura Dent Crane
Hans Christian Andersen	James Allen	Laura Lee Hope
Harold Avery	James Andrews	Laurence Housman
Harold McGrath	James Baldwin	Lawrence Beasley
Harriet Beecher Stowe	James Branch Cabell	Leo Tolstoy
Harry Castlemon	James DeMille	Leonid Andreyev
Harry Coghill	James Joyce	Lewis Carroll
Harry Houidini	James Lane Allen	Lewis Sperry Chafer
Hayden Carruth	James Lane Allen	Lilian Bell
Helent Hunt Jackson	James Oliver Curwood	Lloyd Osbourne
Helen Nicolay	James Oppenheim	Louis Hughes
Hendrik Conscience	James Otis	Louis Tracy
Hendy David Thoreau	James R. Driscoll	Louisa May Alcott
Henri Barbusse	Jane Austen	Lucy Fitch Perkins
Henrik Ibsen	Jane L. Stewart	Lucy Maud Montgomery
Henry Adams	Janet Aldridge	Luther Benson
Henry Ford	Jens Peter Jacobsen	Lydia Miller Middleton
Henry Frost	Jerome K. Jerome	Lyndon Orr
Henry James	John Burroughs	M. Corvus
Henry Jones Ford	John Cournos	M. H. Adams
Henry Seton Merriman	John F. Kennedy	Margaret E. Sangster
Henry W Longfellow	John Gay	Margret Howth
Herbert A. Giles	John Glasworthy	Margaret Vandercook

Margret Penrose
Maria Edgeworth
Maria Thompson Daviess
Mariano Azuela
Marion Polk Angellotti
Mark Overton
Mark Twain
Mary Austin
Mary Catherine Crowley
Mary Cole
Mary Hastings Bradley
Mary Roberts Rinehart
Mary Rowlandson
M. Wollstonecraft Shelley
Maud Lindsay
Max Beerbohm
Myra Kelly
Nathaniel Hawthrone
Nicolo Machiavelli
O. F. Walton
Oscar Wilde
Owen Johnson
P.G. Wodehouse
Paul and Mabel Thorne
Paul G. Tomlinson
Paul Severing
Percy Brebner
Peter B. Kyne
Plato
R. Derby Holmes
R. L. Stevenson
R. S. Ball
Rabindranath Tagore
Rahul Alvares
Ralph Bonehill
Ralph Henry Barbour
Ralph Victor
Ralph Waldo Emmerson
Rene Descartes
Rex Beach

Rex E. Beach
Richard Harding Davis
Richard Jefferies
Richard Le Gallienne
Robert Barr
Robert Frost
Robert Gordon Anderson
Robert L. Drake
Robert Lansing
Robert Lynd
Robert Michael Ballantyne
Robert W. Chambers
Rosa Nouchette Carey
Rudyard Kipling
Samuel B. Allison
Samuel Hopkins Adams
Sarah Bernhardt
Sarah C. Hallowell
Selma Lagerlof
Sherwood Anderson
Sigmund Freud
Standish O'Grady
Stanley Weyman
Stella Benson
Stella M. Francis
Stephen Crane
Stewart Edward White
Stijn Streuvels
Swami Abhedananda
Swami Parmananda
T. S. Ackland
T. S. Arthur
The Princess Der Ling
Thomas A. Janvier
Thomas A Kempis
Thomas Anderton
Thomas Bailey Aldrich
Thomas Bulfinch
Thomas De Quincey
Thomas Dixon

Thomas H. Huxley
Thomas Hardy
Thomas More
Thornton W. Burgess
U. S. Grant
Valentine Williams
Various Authors
Vaughan Kester
Victor Appleton
Victoria Cross
Virginia Woolf
Wadsworth Camp
Walter Camp
Walter Scott
Washington Irving
Wilbur Lawton
Wilkie Collins
Willa Cather
Willard F. Baker
William Dean Howells
William le Queux
W. Makepeace Thackeray
William W. Walter
William Shakespeare
Winston Churchill
Yei Theodora Ozaki
Yogi Ramacharaka
Young E. Allison
Zane Grey